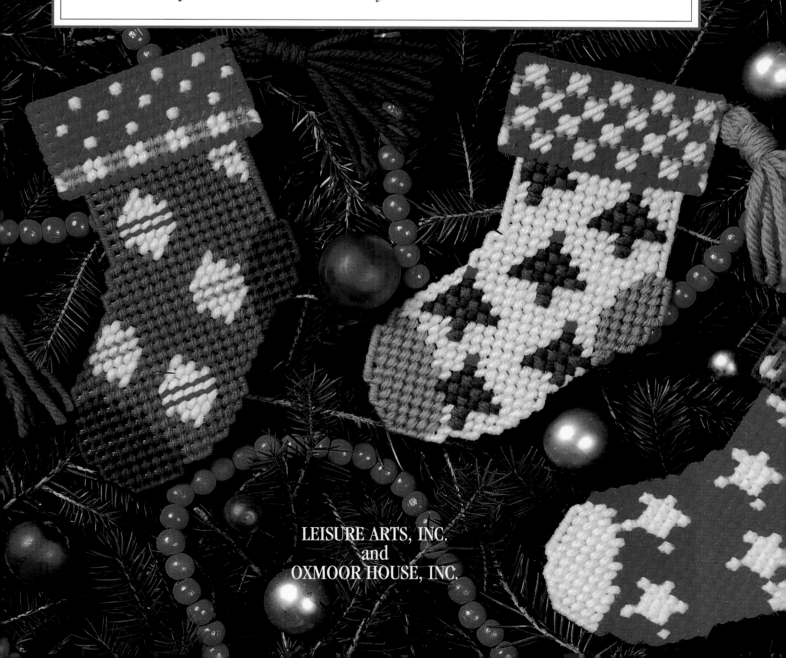

MAKE IT MERRY
IN PLASTIC CANVAS

Make this Christmas the merriest ever with this helpful holiday handbook! It contains lots of wonderful new plastic canvas needlepoint projects — from tree ornaments and coaster sets to festive party favors — to help you fill your home with the spirit of Christmas. There are some thoughtful little gifts for sharing with those who are close to your heart, too. Creating a Christmas your loved ones will always remember has never been easier!

LEISURE ARTS, INC.
and
OXMOOR HOUSE, INC.

MAKE IT MERRY IN PLASTIC CANVAS

EDITORIAL STAFF

Editor-in-Chief: Anne Van Wagner Childs
Executive Director: Sandra Graham Case
Executive Editor: Susan Frantz Wiles
Publications Director: Carla Bentley
Creative Art Director: Gloria Bearden
Production Art Director: Melinda Stout

PRODUCTION
Managing Editor: Teal Lee Elliott
Project Coordinators: Phyllis Miller Boorsma, Michelle Sass Goodrich, Catherine Hubmann, Susan McManus Johnson, and Rhonda Goerke Lombardo
Project Assistant: Kandi Brock Ashford

DESIGN
Design Director: Patricia Wallenfang Sowers

EDITORIAL
Associate Editor: Linda L. Trimble
Senior Editorial Writer: Darla Burdette Kelsay
Editorial Associates: Tammi Williamson Bradley, Robyn Sheffield-Edwards, and Terri Leming Davidson
Copy Editor: Laura Lee Weland

ART
Crafts Art Director: Rhonda Hodge Shelby
Senior Production Artist: Jonathan M. Flaxman
Production Artists: Roberta Aulwes, Mary Ellen Wilhelm, Katie Murphy, Dana Vaughn, Hubrith E. Esters, and Karen L. Wilson
Photography Stylists: Emily Minnick, Christina Tiano, Sondra Daniel, Aurora Huston, and Laura Bushmiaer

BUSINESS STAFF

Publisher: Bruce Akin
Controller: Tom Siebenmorgen
Retail Sales Director: Richard Tignor
Retail Marketing Director: Pam Stebbins
Retail Customer Services Director: Margaret Sweetin
Marketing Manager: Russ Barnett

Executive Director of Marketing and Circulation: Guy A. Crossley
Circulation Manager: Byron L. Taylor
Print Production Manager: Laura Lockhart
Print Production Coordinator: Nancy Reddick Lister

MAKE IT MERRY IN PLASTIC CANVAS
from the *Plastic Canvas Creations* series
Published by Leisure Arts, Inc., and Oxmoor House, Inc.

Library of Congress Catalog Number 94-74355
Hardcover ISBN 0-942237-68-4
Softcover ISBN 0-942237-69-2

TABLE OF CONTENTS

Good News Nativity

In this tranquil Nativity scene, a star held by two angels proclaims the good news of the Savior's birth. The inspirational set will help you celebrate the true meaning of Christmas.

FOR UNTO YOU
IS BORN THIS DAY
IN THE CITY OF
DAVID A SAVIOUR,
WHICH IS CHRIST
THE LORD.

NATIVITY

Skill Level: Intermediate
Size: 11¾"w x 13"h x 2¼"d
Supplies: Worsted weight yarn or Needloft® Plastic Canvas Yarn (refer to color keys), DMC embroidery floss (refer to color key), five 10½" x 13½" sheets of 7 mesh plastic canvas, one 8⅛" x 10⅞" sheet of 14 mesh plastic canvas (for Star only), #16 and #24 tapestry needles, polyester fiberfill, aquarium gravel, sealable plastic bag, tissue paper, nylon line, and clear-drying craft glue
Stitches Used: Backstitch, Cashmere Stitch, Checkered Scotch Stitch, French Knot, Gobelin Stitch, Overcast Stitch, and Tent Stitch

BABY JESUS

Size: 3⅝"w x 3½"h
Instructions: Follow charts and use required stitches to work Baby Jesus pieces. Use yarn color to match stitching area to join Front to Back. Refer to photo and use tan to tack Hay to Front and Back.

MARY

Size: 4¼"w x 5½"h
Instructions: Follow charts and use required stitches to work Mary pieces. Refer to photo and use rose to tack Arm to Front. Use yarn color to match stitching area to join Front to Back. Lightly stuff opening at bottom of stitched piece with tissue paper.

JOSEPH

Size: 3½"w x 7½"h
Instructions: Follow charts and use required stitches to work Joseph pieces. Use yarn color to match stitching area to join Front to Back. Lightly stuff opening at bottom of stitched piece with tissue paper.

ANGELS

Size: 4¾"w x 5½"h
Instructions: Follow charts and use required stitches to work Angel pieces. Refer to photo and use burgundy to tack Arm to Front. Use yarn color to match stitching area to join Front to Back.

STAR

Size: 4⅝"w x 5½"h
Instructions: Follow chart and use required stitches to work Star Front. Use six strands of embroidery floss for Tent Stitches and three strands for Backstitch and French Knot. Complete background with gold embroidery floss Tent Stitches as indicated on chart. Turn Back over. Work Back with gold embroidery floss Tent Stitches. Use gold embroidery floss to join Front to Back.

STABLE

Size: 9"w x 9¾"h x 2½"d
Instructions: Follow charts and use required stitches to work Stable pieces, using a double thickness of plastic canvas for all pieces except Posts. For Floor Bottom, cut two pieces of plastic canvas 57 x 14 threads each. (**Note:** Floor Bottom is not worked.) Use brown for all joining. For Post #1, match like symbols to join Post Sides A, B, C, and E. For Post #2, match like symbols to join Post Sides A, B, D, and F. Match ▼'s to join Post #1 to Floor Top. Match *'s to join Post #2 to Floor Top. Join Floor Front and Floor Back to Floor Ends along short edges. Join Floor Top to Floor Front, Back, and Ends. Insert bag of aquarium gravel in Floor. Fill in remaining space with polyester fiberfill. Join Floor Bottom to Floor Front, Back, and Ends. Join Roof pieces along unworked edges. Refer to photo to tack Roof Front to Roof. Refer to photo to tack Roof to Posts. Refer to photo and use nylon line to tack Angels to Star. Refer to photo and use nylon line to tack Angels and Star to Stable.

Nativity designed by Karen Wood.

NL	COLOR		NL	COLOR		NL	COLOR
00	black - 7 yds		48	dk blue - 2 yds		33	blue - 20 yds
03	burgundy - 40 yds		56	flesh - 7 yds		41	white - 10 yds
05	rose - 10 yds						
10	brown - 85 yds						
19	yellow - 8 yds						

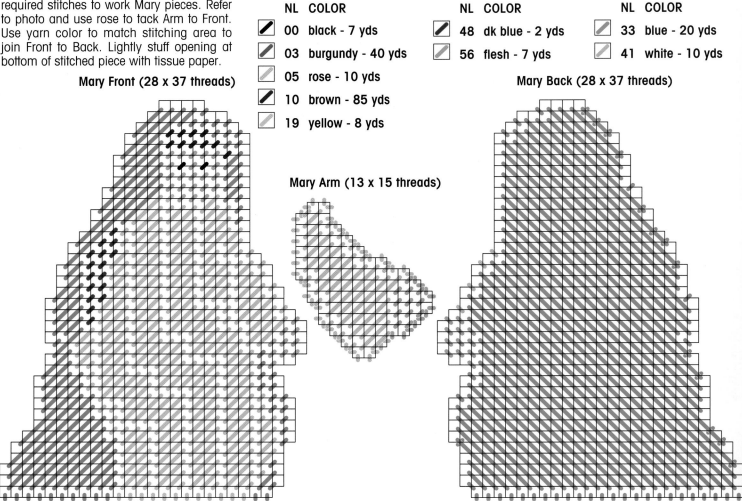

Mary Front (28 x 37 threads)

Mary Arm (13 x 15 threads)

Mary Back (28 x 37 threads)

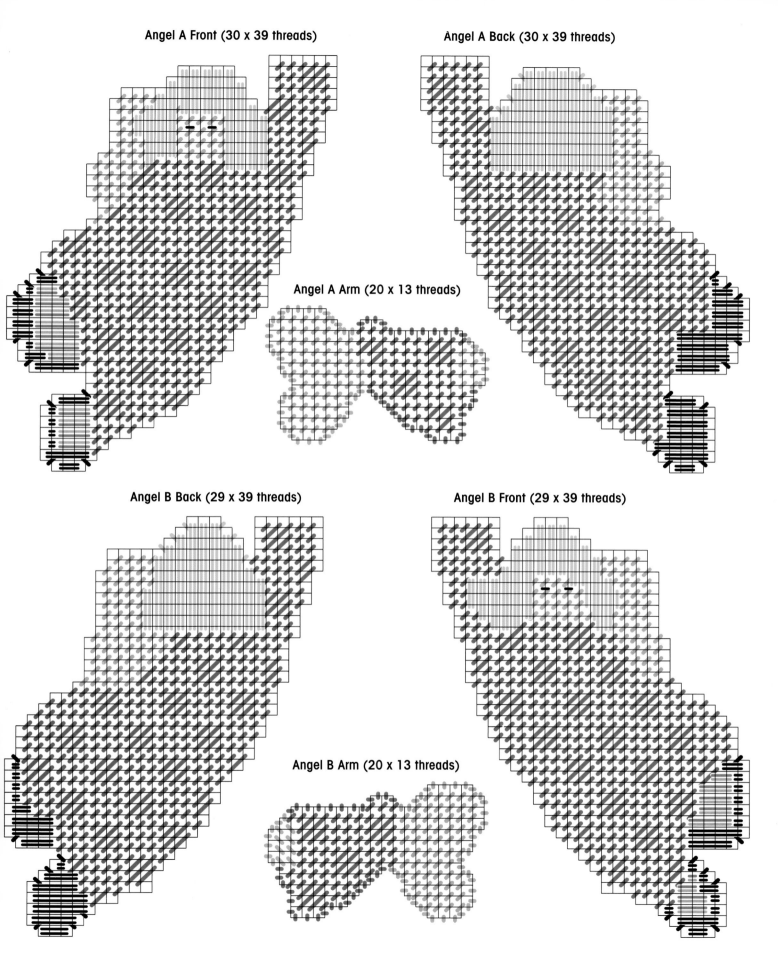

Angel A Front (30 x 39 threads)

Angel A Back (30 x 39 threads)

Angel A Arm (20 x 13 threads)

Angel B Back (29 x 39 threads)

Angel B Front (29 x 39 threads)

Angel B Arm (20 x 13 threads)

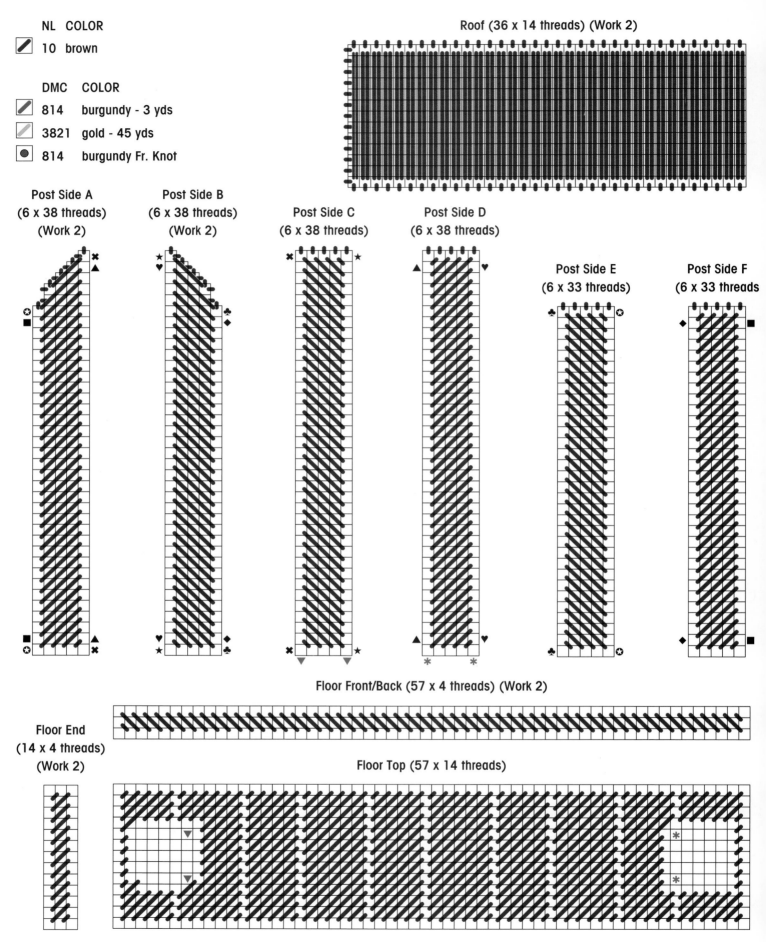

NL COLOR

10 brown

DMC COLOR

814 burgundy - 3 yds

3821 gold - 45 yds

814 burgundy Fr. Knot

Roof (36 x 14 threads) (Work 2)

Post Side A
(6 x 38 threads)
(Work 2)

Post Side B
(6 x 38 threads)
(Work 2)

Post Side C
(6 x 38 threads)

Post Side D
(6 x 38 threads)

Post Side E
(6 x 33 threads)

Post Side F
(6 x 33 threads

Floor Front/Back (57 x 4 threads) (Work 2)

Floor End
(14 x 4 threads)
(Work 2)

Floor Top (57 x 14 threads)

Roof Front (61 x 29 threads)

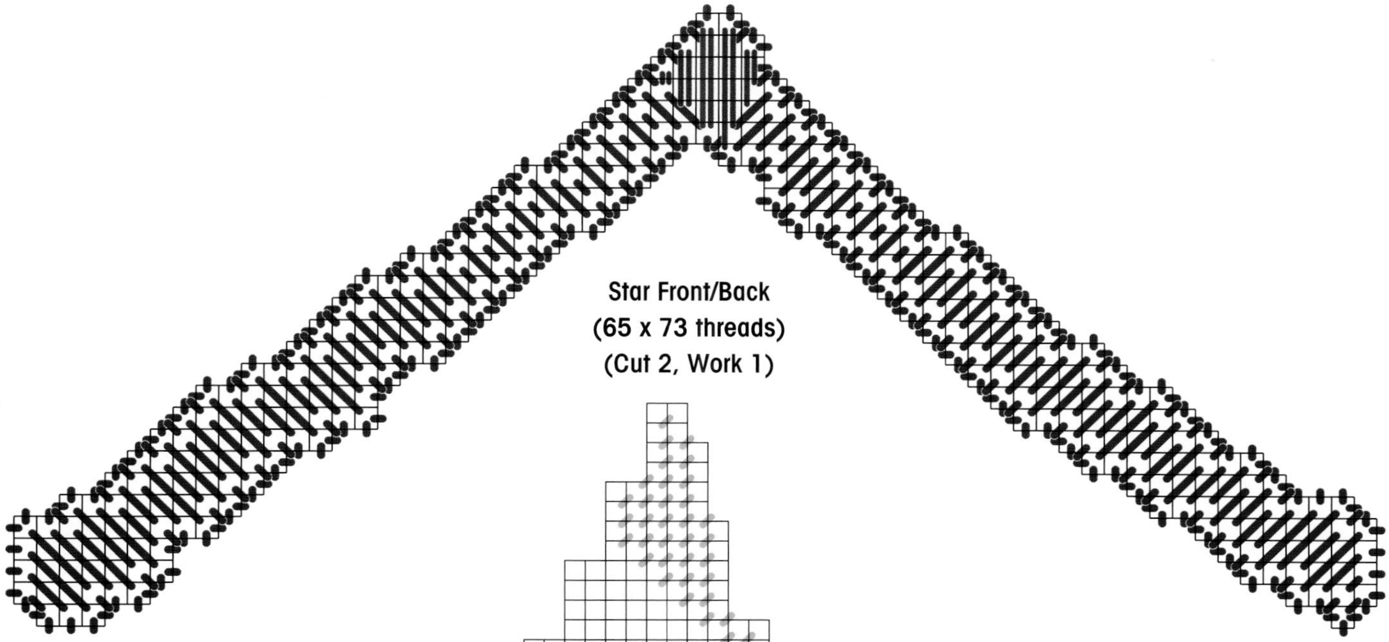

**Star Front/Back
(65 x 73 threads)
(Cut 2, Work 1)**

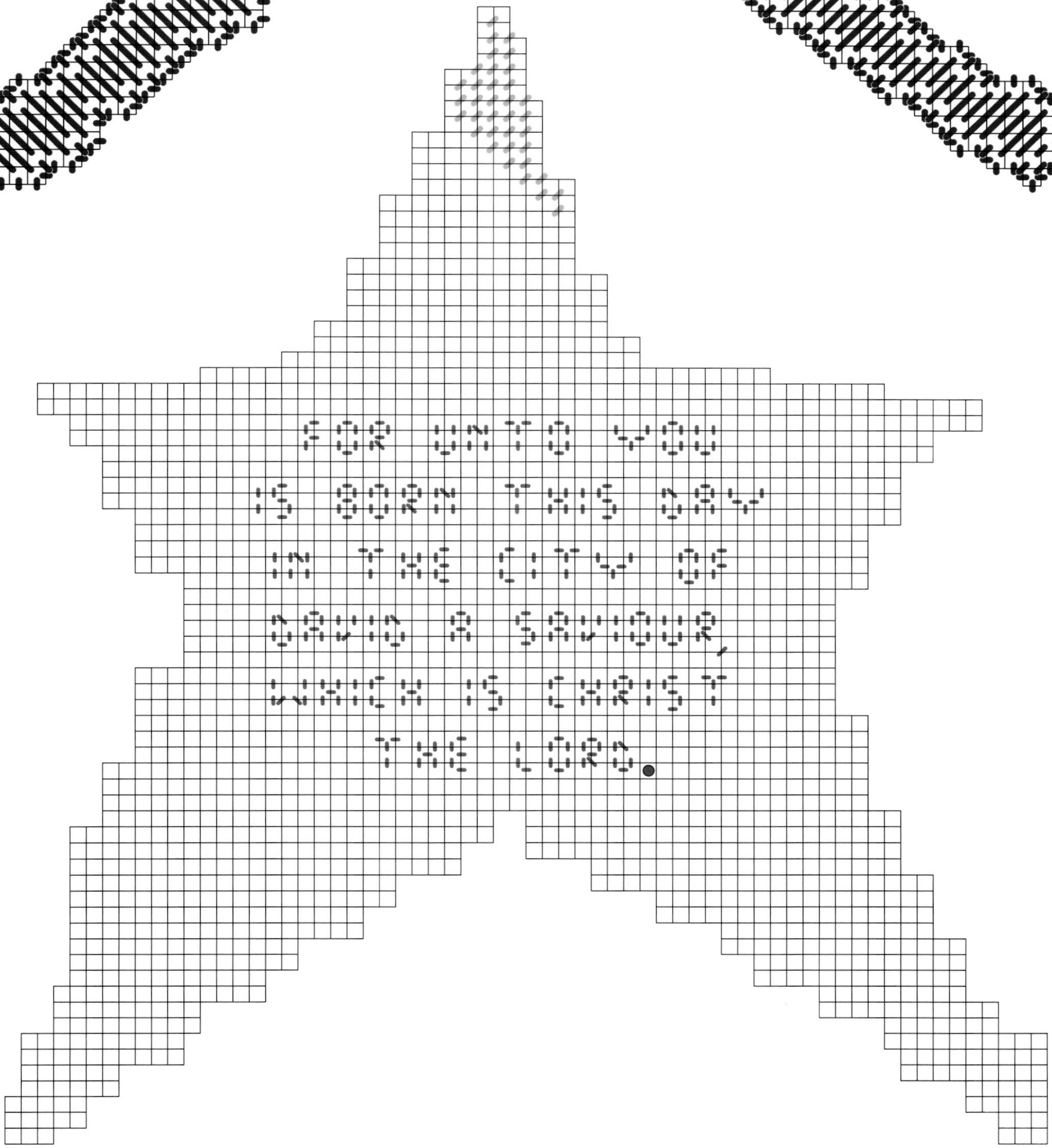

FOR UNTO YOU
IS BORN THIS DAY
IN THE CITY OF
DAVID A SAVIOUR,
WHICH IS CHRIST
THE LORD.

9

NL	COLOR
00	black
03	burgundy
10	brown
11	tan - 8 yds
35	lt blue - 2 yds
39	ecru - 6 yds
53	green - 20 yds
56	flesh

Baby Jesus Front (24 x 23 threads)

Baby Jesus Back (24 x 23 threads)

Joseph Front (23 x 50 threads)

Hay (24 x 12 threads) (Work 2)

Joseph Back (23 x 50 threads)

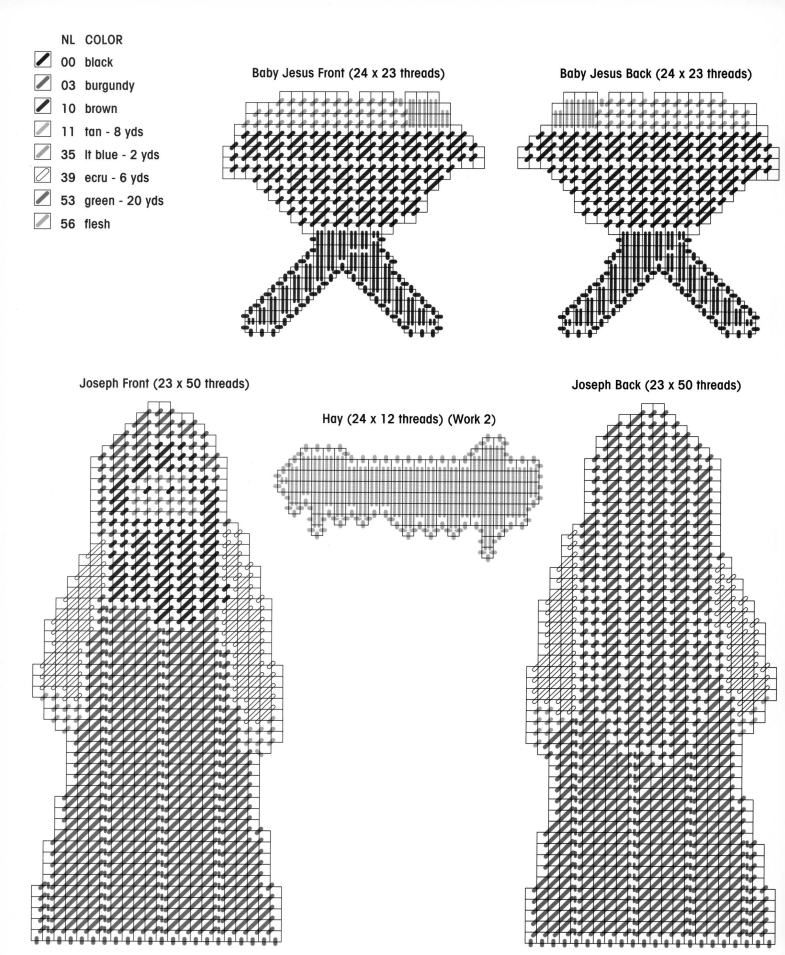

Photo Keepsake Ornament

Opening like a greeting card, our festive frame makes a precious ornament. What a merry way to display your favorite wallet-size photo!

PHOTO FRAME ORNAMENT
Skill Level: Beginner
Size: 5¼"w x 3⅜"h
Supplies: Needloft® Plastic Canvas Yarn or worsted weight yarn (refer to color key), one 10½" x 13½" sheet of 7 mesh plastic canvas, #16 tapestry needle, white felt, nylon line, #26 tapestry needle (for working with nylon line), and clear-drying craft glue
Stitches Used: Gobelin Stitch, Overcast Stitch, and Tent Stitch
Instructions: Follow charts and use required stitches to work Ornament pieces. For Back, cut a piece of plastic canvas 18 x 23 threads. Work Back with white Tent Stitches. Use red for all joining. Refer to photo to join Front to Back along unworked edge of Front. Join Frame to Back along unworked edges. Refer to photo to glue felt to wrong side of Front. For hanger, thread 8" of nylon line through stitched piece. Tie ends together in a knot 3" above Ornament.

Photo Frame Ornament designed by Mary T. Cosgrove.

NL	COLOR
02	Christmas red - 5 yds
28	Christmas green - 6 yds
41	white - 15 yds

Frame (18 x 23 threads)

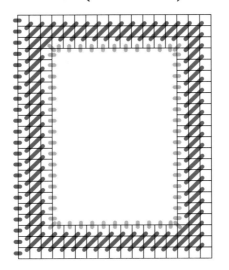

Front (18 x 23 threads)

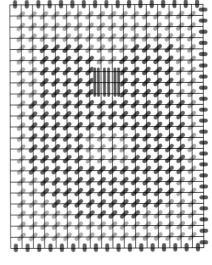

FESTIVE FAVORS

Filled with a sweet surprise or a tiny trinket, these cute projects make festive favors — and they double as tree ornaments! They're easy enough for beginners to make, and each one works up quickly so you can give one to everyone on your list.

For Phil

FAVOR ORNAMENTS

Skill Level: Beginner
Approx Size: 2½"w x 3½"h x 1¼"d each
Supplies: Worsted weight yarn or Needloft® Plastic Canvas Yarn (refer to color key), one 10½" x 13½" sheet of 7 mesh plastic canvas, #16 tapestry needle, 6" of gold cord, two 8" lengths of ¼"w red picot satin ribbon, one 5mm yellow pom-pom, four 7mm yellow pom-poms, and clear-drying craft glue
Stitches Used: Cashmere Stitch, Gobelin Stitch, Overcast Stitch, and Tent Stitch
Tote Bag Ornament Instructions: Follow charts and use required stitches to work Ornament pieces, leaving stitches in shaded areas unworked. Match ✖'s and work stitches in shaded areas to join Handles to Front and Back. Use red for all joining. Match ▲'s to join Side A pieces to Side B pieces. Refer to photo to join Front and Back to Sides. Join Front, Back, and Sides to Bottom.

NL	COLOR
✏ 02	Christmas red
✏ 27	green
✏ 41	white

Poinsettia Basket Front & Back (16 x 43 threads)

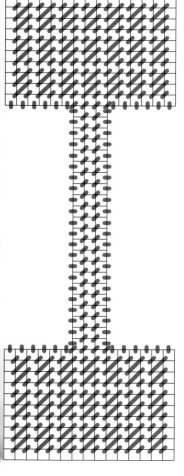

Heart Pocket Ornament Instructions: Follow charts and use required stitches to work Ornament pieces. For handle, thread ends of gold cord through Back at ✦'s. Tie each end of cord in a knot on wrong side of Back and trim ends. Refer to photo for yarn color used to join Front to Back along unworked edges.

Heart Pocket Front (22 x 22 threads)

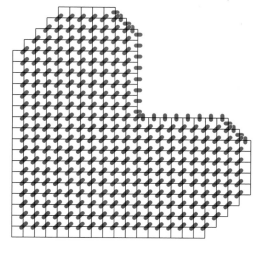

Heart Pocket Back (22 x 22 threads)

Poinsettia Basket Ornament Instructions: Follow charts and use required stitches to work Ornament pieces. Use green for all joining. Join Sides to Front & Back. For Bottom, cut a piece of plastic canvas 16 x 10 threads. (**Note:** Bottom is not worked.) Join Bottom to Front & Back and Sides. Tie each length of ribbon in a bow and trim ends. Refer to photo to glue Petals to Front. Glue pom-poms to Petals. Glue bows to Sides.

Tote Bag Ornament designed by Debra Gann.
Heart Pocket Ornament designed by Rose D. Munz.
Poinsettia Basket Ornament designed by Sandy and Honey for Studio M.

Tote Bag Front/Back (13 x 17 threads) (Work 2)

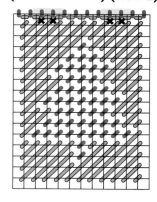

Tote Bag Bottom (13 x 8 threads)

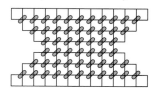

Poinsettia Basket Side (10 x 11 threads) (Work 2)

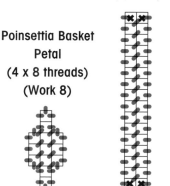

Poinsettia Basket Petal (4 x 8 threads) (Work 8)

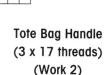

Tote Bag Handle (3 x 17 threads) (Work 2)

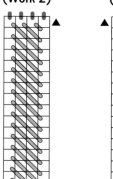

Tote Bag Side A (5 x 17 threads) (Work 2)

Tote Bag Side B (5 x 17 threads) (Work 2)

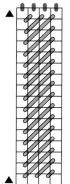

Olde World Santa

In this portrait, kindness and compassion radiate from the twinkling eyes of the gentle old soul we've come to know as Santa Claus. Clad in a hooded red robe, he also makes a stunning tree topper when stitched on 10 mesh canvas.

SANTA FRAMED PIECE

Skill Level: Intermediate

Size: 13 5/8"w x 17"h

Supplies: Paternayan® Persian Yarn or worsted weight yarn (refer to color key), brown embroidery floss, one 13 5/8" x 21 5/8" sheet of 7 mesh plastic canvas, #16 tapestry needle, and frame

Stitches Used: Backstitch, French Knot, Smyrna Cross Stitch, and Tent Stitch

Instructions: Cut a piece of plastic canvas 91 x 114 threads. Center design on piece of plastic canvas. (**Note:** Design is 71 stitches wide and 94 stitches high.) When color key indicates embroidery floss, use six strands. Follow chart and use required stitches to work Top Section. Follow chart and use required stitches to work Bottom Section below Top Section. Use 501 blue Tent Stitches to work background. Insert stitched piece into frame. (**Note:** Photo model was custom framed.)

SANTA TREE TOPPER

Skill Level: Intermediate

Size: 7 3/8"w x 9 5/8"h

Supplies: Paternayan® Persian Yarn or worsted weight yarn (refer to color key), brown embroidery floss, one 10 1/2" x 13 1/2" sheet of 10 mesh plastic canvas, #20 tapestry needle, nylon line, and #26 tapestry needle (for working with nylon line)

Stitches Used: Backstitch, French Knot, Overcast Stitch, Smyrna Cross Stitch, and Tent Stitch

Instructions: Use design thread count to center design on sheet of 10 mesh plastic canvas (101 x 137 threads). (**Note:** Design is 71 stitches wide and 94 stitches high.) When color key indicates embroidery floss, use three strands. Follow chart and use required stitches to work Top Section. Follow chart and use required stitches to work Bottom Section below Top Section. Use chart as a guide to cut out Santa, leaving one unworked thread around entire stitched area. Use color to match stitching area to work background color stitches. Use color to match stitching area to work Overcast Stitches to cover unworked edges. For loops, cut three pieces of plastic canvas 22 x 7 threads each. Use nylon line to attach short edges of loops to wrong side of Santa at ★'s.

PTN	COLOR
864	dk peach
874	dk flesh
875	lt flesh
900	vy dk red
940	dk red
969	red
972	lt red
	background color
	brown embroidery floss
260	white Fr. Knot

PTN	COLOR
201	dk grey
202	grey
237	lt grey
260	white
484	brown
491	flesh
494	vy lt flesh
501	blue
610	green
611	lt green

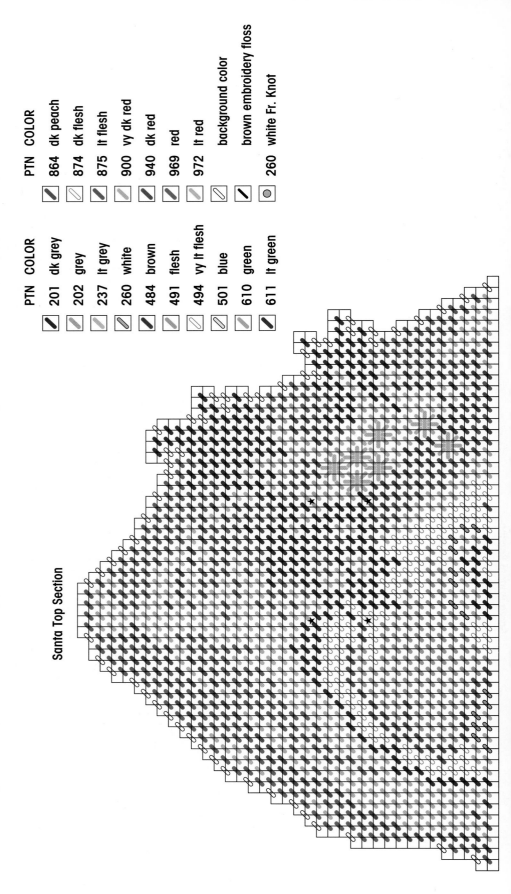

Santa Top Section

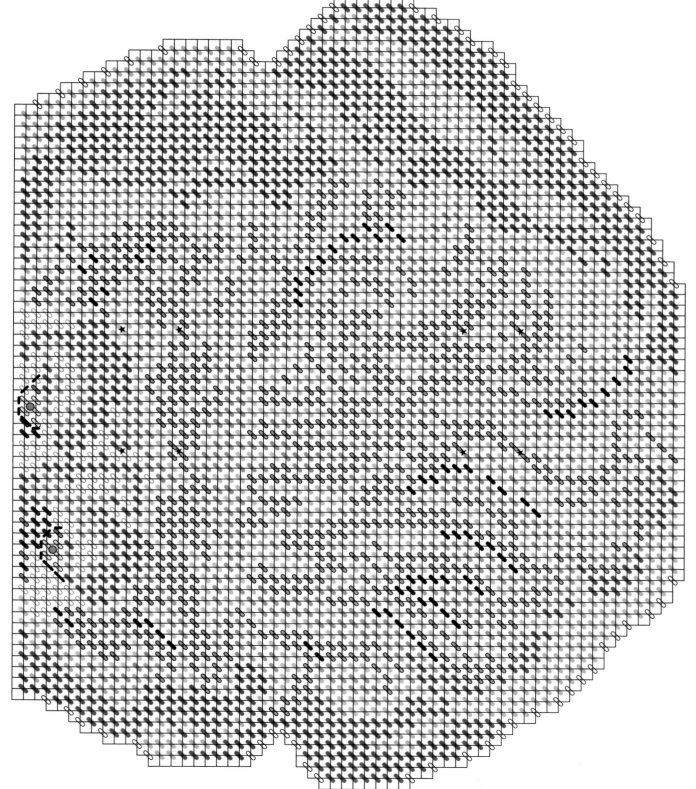

"Beary" Merry Ornaments

Like your childhood teddy, these ornaments are destined to become cherished favorites. They make adorable tree-trimmers, or you can use them to add holiday greetings to your gift packages. However you choose to display them, you're sure to have a "beary" Merry Christmas!

TEDDY BEAR ORNAMENTS

Skill Level: Beginner

Approx Size: 3"w x 4¼"h each

Supplies: Worsted weight yarn or Needloft® Plastic Canvas Yarn (refer to color key), DMC 6-strand embroidery floss (refer to color key), one 10½" x 13½" sheet of 7 mesh plastic canvas, #16 tapestry needle, nylon line, and #26 tapestry needle (for working with nylon line)

Stitches Used: Backstitch, Cross Stitch, French Knot, Gobelin Stitch, Overcast Stitch, and Tent Stitch

Instructions: Follow charts and use required stitches to work Ornament pieces. Refer to photo and use brown to tack Sign to Bear. For hanger, thread 8" of nylon line through stitched piece. Tie ends together in a knot 3" above Ornament.

Teddy Bear Ornaments designed by Joyce Levitt.

NL	COLOR
02	red - 5 yds
15	brown - 7 yds
27	green - 6 yds
41	white - 5 yds
43	lt brown - 1 yd

DMC	COLOR
310	black - 3 yds
666	red - 2 yds
310	black Fr. Knot

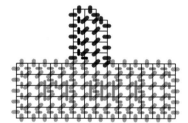

Joy Sign
(12 x 11 threads)

Noel Sign
(11 x 12 threads)

Peace Sign
(15 x 11 threads)

Joy Bear
(16 x 30 threads)

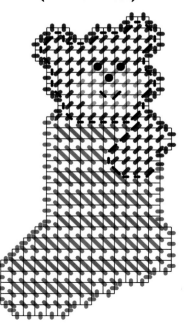

Noel Bear
(16 x 28 threads)

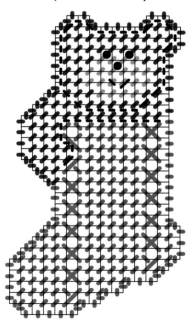

Peace Bear
(16 x 28 threads)

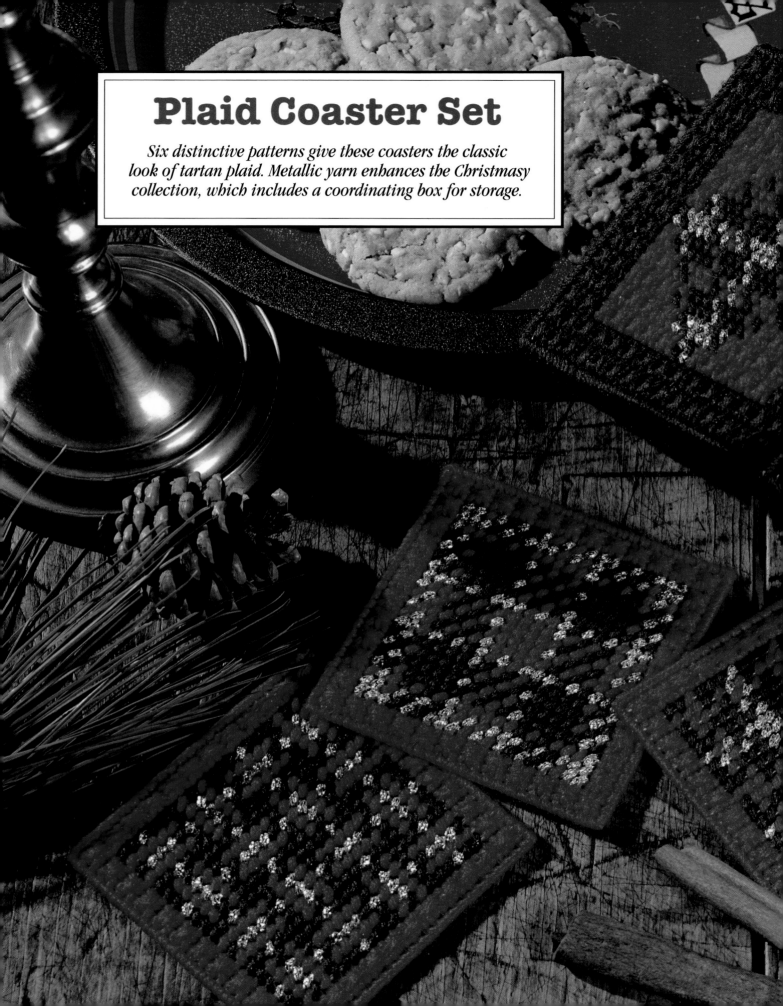

Plaid Coaster Set

Six distinctive patterns give these coasters the classic look of tartan plaid. Metallic yarn enhances the Christmasy collection, which includes a coordinating box for storage.

PLAID COASTER SET

Skill Level: Beginner
Supplies: Worsted weight yarn or Needloft® Plastic Canvas Yarn (refer to color key), metallic gold yarn, two 10¹/₂" x 13¹/₂" sheets of 7 mesh plastic canvas, #16 tapestry needle, cork or felt (optional), and clear-drying craft glue
Stitches Used: Overcast Stitch, Smyrna Cross Stitch, and Tent Stitch

Holder Size: 4⁷/₈"w x 2⁵/₈"h x 4⁷/₈"d
Holder Instructions: Follow charts and use required stitches to work Holder pieces. Use green for all joining. Join Top Sides along short edges. Join Top to Top Sides. Join Bottom Sides along short edges. Join Bottom to Bottom Sides.

Coaster Size: 3⁷/₈"w x 3⁷/₈"h each
Coaster Instructions: Follow charts and use required stitches to work Coasters. For backing, cut cork or felt slightly smaller than Coaster and glue to wrong side of stitched piece.

Plaid Coaster Set designed by Marion Peairs.

NL	COLOR
✎ 01	red - 66 yds
✎ 28	green - 69 yds
✎	metallic gold - 28 yds

Bottom Side (30 x 16 threads) (Work 4)

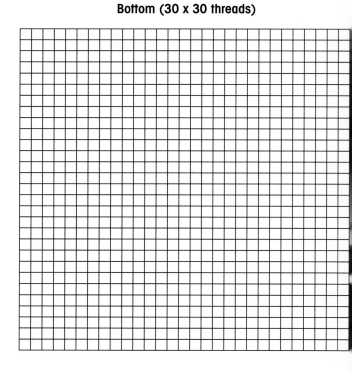

Top Side (32 x 6 threads) (Work 4)

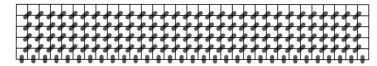

Top (32 x 32 threads)

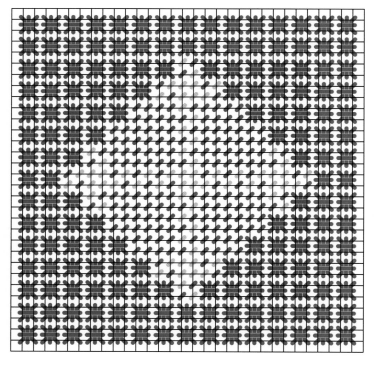

Bottom (30 x 30 threads)

22

Coaster A (26 x 26 threads)

Coaster B (26 x 26 threads)

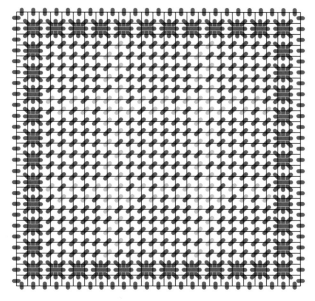

Coaster C (26 x 26 threads)

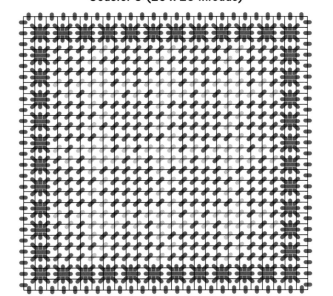

Coaster D (26 x 26 threads)

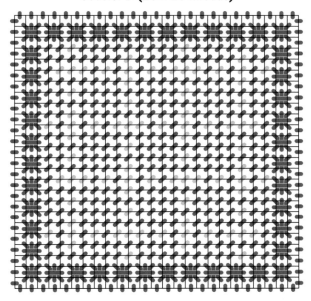

Coaster E (26 x 26 threads)

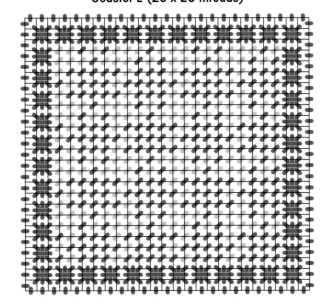

Coaster F (26 x 26 threads)

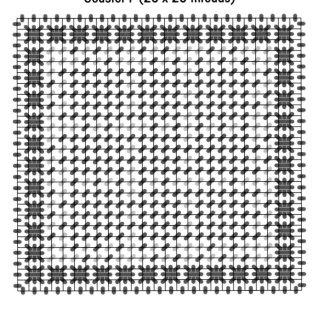

23

GOODIE SANTA

Ready for a Merry Christmas hug, this plump Santa comes apart to reveal a belly full of candy or other sweet surprises. The jolly old elf makes an adorable party favor, or he can accompany a special holiday gift. He's sure to bring a bundle of smiles!

SANTA GOODIE HOLDER

Skill Level: Beginner
Size: 4"w x 5¼"h x 3"d
Supplies: Worsted weight yarn or Needloft® Plastic Canvas Yarn (refer to color key), one 10½" x 13½" sheet of 7 mesh plastic canvas, and #16 tapestry needle
Stitches Used: Backstitch, Cross Stitch, Fringe, Gobelin Stitch, Overcast Stitch, and Tent Stitch
Instructions: Follow charts and use required stitches to work Santa Goodie Holder pieces. Use color to match stitching area for all joining. Refer to photo to join Bottom Front and Bottom Back to Bottom Sides. Join Bottom Front, Back, and Sides to Feet along unworked threads. With wrong sides together, join Face Front to Face Back, leaving area between ▲'s unworked. Match ▲'s to join Face Front and Back to Neck. Refer to photo to join Top Front and Top Back to Top Sides. Join Neck to Top Front, Back, and Sides along unworked edges. With wrong sides together, join Arm A to Arm B. Repeat for remaining Arm pieces. Refer to photo to tack Arms to Top Sides. Refer to photo to separate Fringe into plies and to trim.

Santa Goodie Holder designed by Jack Peatman for Luvlee Designs.

NL	COLOR
00	black - 11 yds
01	dk red - 1 yd
02	red - 13 yds
19	yellow - 1 yd
28	green - 1 yd
38	grey - 1 yd
	grey 2-ply
41	white - 10 yds
56	flesh - 1 yd
41	white Fringe

Face Front
(15 x 13 threads)

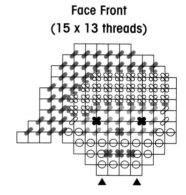

Face Back
(15 x 13 threads)

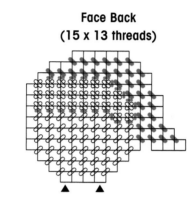

Top Front
(13 x 13 threads)

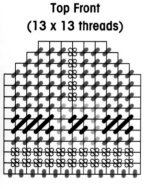

Top Back
(13 x 13 threads)

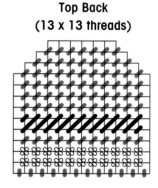

Arm A
(8 x 10 threads)
(Work 2)

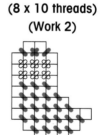

Arm B
(8 x 10 threads)
(Work 2)

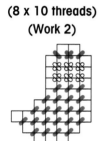

Neck
(7 x 7 threads)

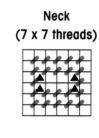

Feet (15 x 20 threads)

Bottom Front/Back
(11 x 13 threads) (Work 2)

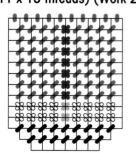

Bottom Side
(11 x 13 threads) (Work 2)

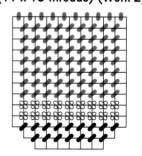

Top Side
(13 x 13 threads) (Work 2)

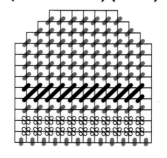

25

Ornamental Stockings

Make your Christmas bright and gay with this merry collection of Christmas stockings. Finished with handmade tassels, the ornaments feature six holiday patterns that capture cherished images of the Yuletide season.

STOCKING ORNAMENTS

Skill Level: Beginner

Size: 4¼"w x 5¾"h each

Supplies: Worsted weight yarn or Needloft® Plastic Canvas Yarn (refer to color key), two 10½" x 13½" sheets of 7 mesh plastic canvas, #16 tapestry needle, nylon line, and #26 tapestry needle (for working with nylon line)

Stitches Used: Backstitch, Cross Stitch, Gobelin Stitch, Mosaic Stitch, Overcast Stitch, and Tent Stitch

Instructions: Follow chart and use required stitches to work Ornament. For tassel, cut ten 5" lengths and one 20" length of yarn. Fold 5" lengths of yarn in half. Make a small loop on one end of 20" length of yarn. Refer to **Fig. A** to wrap 20" length of yarn around folded 5" lengths several times, covering almost all of the loop. Thread end of 20" length through loop **(Fig. B)**. Pull other end of 20" length until loop disappears under wrapped area **(Fig. C)**. Trim end at top close to wrapped area. Refer to photo to attach tassel to Ornament. For hanger, thread 8" of nylon line through stitched piece. Tie ends together in a knot 3" above Ornament.

Stocking Ornaments designed by Kooler Design Studio, Inc.

Fig. A

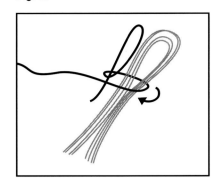

Fig. C

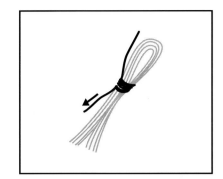

Fig. B

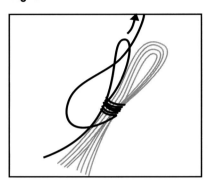

NL	COLOR
02	red - 17 yds
13	brown - 1 yd
20	yellow - 16 yds
23	lt green - 10 yds
27	green - 16 yds
35	blue - 11 yds
39	ecru - 15 yds

Ornament #1 (27 x 38 threads)

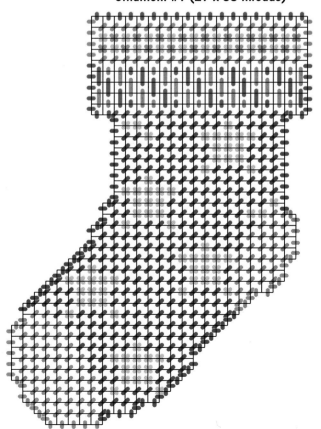

Ornament #2 (27 x 38 threads)

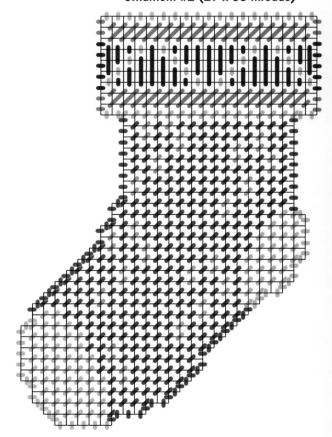

Ornament #3 (27 x 38 threads)

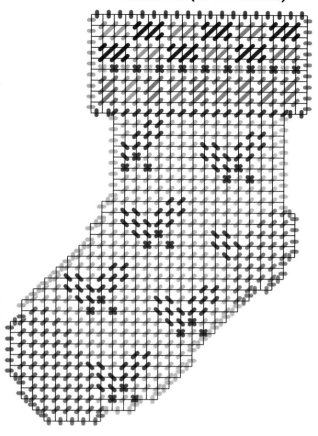

Ornament #4 (27 x 38 threads)

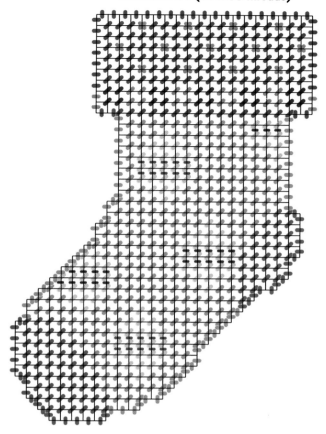

Ornament #5 (27 x 38 threads)

Ornament #6 (27 x 38 threads)

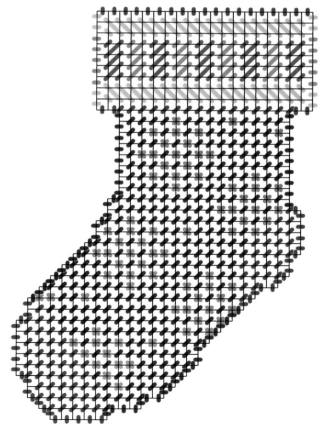

29

Noel Santa

Holding a happy holiday message, this jovial Santa hangs on your door to greet holiday guests. White French knots trim his jaunty red suit with "fur," and fringe gives the kind-hearted gentleman his woolly white beard.

NOEL SANTA DOOR DECORATION

Skill Level: Intermediate
Size: 13½"w x 19"h
Supplies: Worsted weight yarn or Needloft® Plastic Canvas Yarn (refer to color keys), three 10½" x 13½" sheets of 7 mesh plastic canvas, #16 tapestry needle, sawtooth hanger, and clear-drying craft glue or glue gun and glue sticks
Stitches Used: Backstitch, French Knot, Fringe, Gobelin Stitch, Overcast Stitch, and Tent Stitch
Instructions: Follow charts and use required stitches to work Noel Santa Door Decoration pieces, leaving stitches in shaded areas unworked. Refer to photo and match ▲'s to place Top on Bottom. Work stitches in shaded areas to join Top to Bottom. Match ✦'s and use color to match stitching area to join Hat to Top. Refer to photo to glue Arm A to Top. Refer to photo to glue Arm B to wrong side of Top. Refer to photo to trim Fringe. Glue Mustache to Top. For Noel string, cut a 28" length each of red yarn and white yarn. Tie yarn lengths in a knot close to one end. Twist yarn lengths together and tie remaining ends in a knot. Refer to photo and use white to tack ends of Noel string to Arms. Refer to photo and use blue Overcast Stitches to join unworked edges of Letters to twisted yarn. For hanger, glue sawtooth hanger to wrong side of stitched piece.

Noel Santa Door Decoration designed by Joyce Levitt.

NL	COLOR
✏ 00	black - 21 yds
✏	black 2-ply
✏ 01	dk red - 46 yds
✏ 02	red - 20 yds
✏ 17	gold - 3 yds
✏ 35	blue - 11 yds
✏ 41	white - 268 yds
✏ 56	flesh - 11 yds
◉ 41	white Fr. Knot
○ 41	white Fringe

Hat (44 x 30 threads)

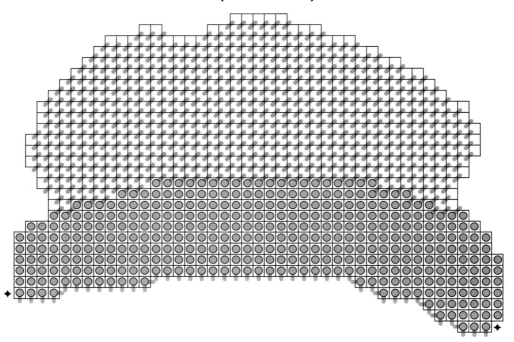

Mustache (20 x 9 threads)

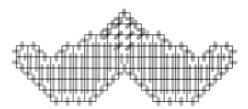

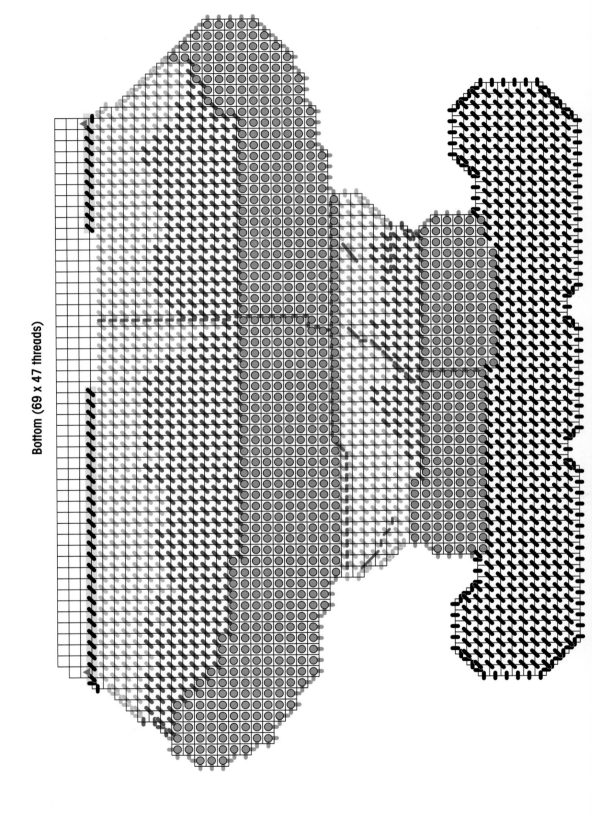

Bottom (69 x 47 threads)

NL	COLOR
00	black
	black 2-ply
01	dk red
02	red

NL	COLOR
27	green - 9 yds
35	blue
41	white
41	white Fr. Knot

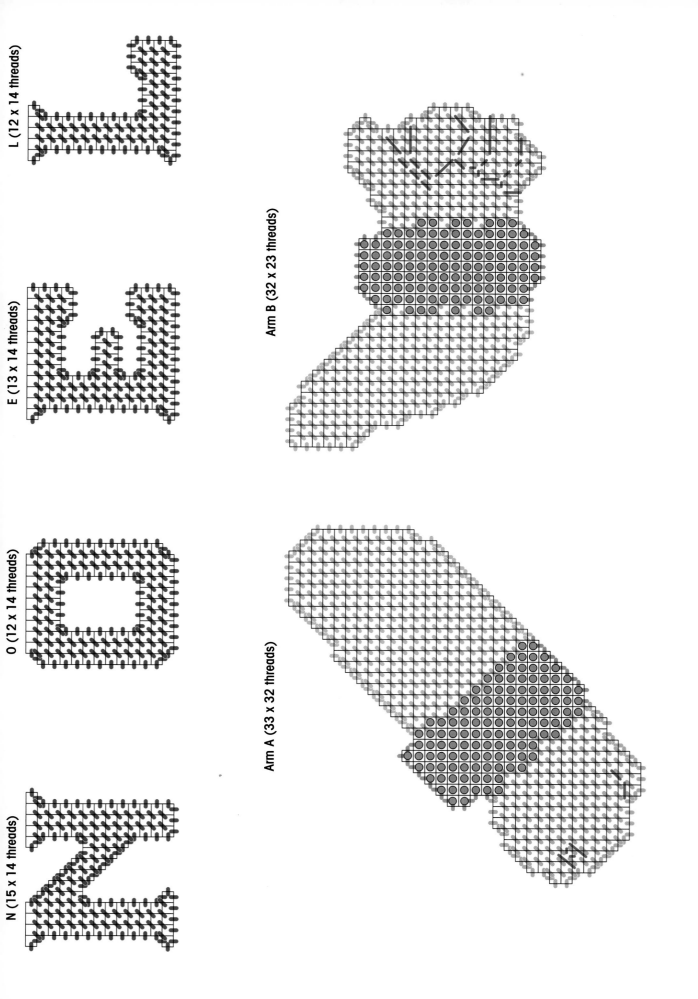

L (12 x 14 threads)

E (13 x 14 threads)

O (12 x 14 threads)

N (15 x 14 threads)

Arm B (32 x 23 threads)

Arm A (33 x 32 threads)

Cheery Set

Symbols of friendship and hospitality, holly wreaths lend cheer to this colorful Christmas ensemble. Metallic gold cord adds sparkle to the set, which includes a bookend, a centerpiece container, a tissue box cover, a mug, and a coaster.

WREATH SET

Skill Level: Beginner

Supplies For Entire Set: Worsted weight yarn or Needloft® Plastic Canvas Yarn (refer to color key), metallic gold cord, three 10½" x 13½" sheets of 7 mesh plastic canvas, one 13½" x 21½" sheet of 7 mesh plastic canvas, one 9½" dia plastic canvas circle, #16 tapestry needle, white Crafter's Pride® Stitch-A-Mug™, brick, plastic wrap, cork or felt, and clear-drying craft glue

Stitches Used: Cross Stitch, Gobelin Stitch, Overcast Stitch, Scotch Stitch, and Tent Stitch

CONTAINER

Size: 3⅝"h x 6" dia

Instructions: For Container Side, cut a piece of plastic canvas 125 x 24 threads. Follow chart and use required stitches to work Side, leaving shaded areas unworked. Refer to photo to continue pattern. Complete background with white Tent Stitches as indicated on chart. For Bottom, cut twelve threads from outer edge of 9½" dia plastic canvas circle. (**Note:** Bottom is not worked.) Match ▲'s and work stitches in shaded areas to join ends of Side, forming a cylinder. Use metallic gold cord to join Side to Bottom. Use metallic gold cord Overcast Stitches to cover unworked edge.

DOORSTOP

Size: 8½"w x 4¼"h x 2½"d

(**Note:** Fits an 8"w x 3⅝"h x 2⅛"d brick.)

Instructions: Follow charts and use required stitches to work Doorstop pieces. Complete backgrounds with white Tent Stitches as indicated on chart. Use red for all joining. Join Long Sides to Short Sides along short edges. Join Front to Sides. Wrap brick with plastic wrap and insert into Doorstop. Join Back to Sides.

TISSUE BOX COVER

Size: 4¾"w x 5¾"h x 4¾"d

(**Note:** Fits a 4¼"w x 5¼"h x 4¼"d boutique tissue box.)

Instructions: Follow charts and use required stitches to work Tissue Box Cover pieces. Complete backgrounds with white Tent Stitches as indicated on charts. Use red for all joining. Join Sides along long edges. Join Top to Sides.

MUG INSERT

Size: 3½"h x 3⅛" dia

Instructions: Follow chart and use required stitches to work Mug Insert. Complete background with white Tent Stitches as indicated on chart. Use metallic gold cord to join short edges, forming a cylinder. Place Mug Insert into Stitch-A-Mug™, aligning joined edges with mug handle. Remove stitched piece before washing mug.

COASTER

Size: 3¾"w x 3⅝"h

Instructions: Follow chart and use required stitches to work Coaster. Complete background with white Tent Stitches as indicated on chart. For backing, cut cork or felt slightly smaller than Coaster and glue to wrong side of stitched piece.

Wreath Set designed by Ann Townsend.

NL	COLOR
✎	02 Christmas red
✎	27 holly
✎	41 white
✎	metallic gold cord

Coaster (25 x 24 threads)

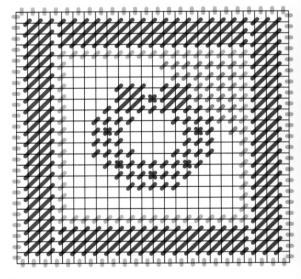

Container Side (125 x 24 threads)

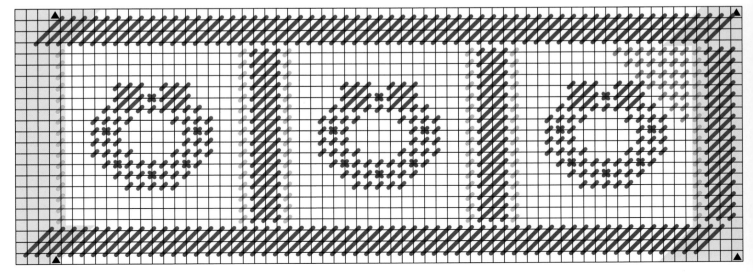

Doorstop Short Side
(27 x 17 threads) (Work 2)

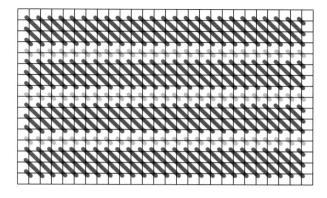

Doorstop Long Side
(17 x 57 threads) (Work 2)

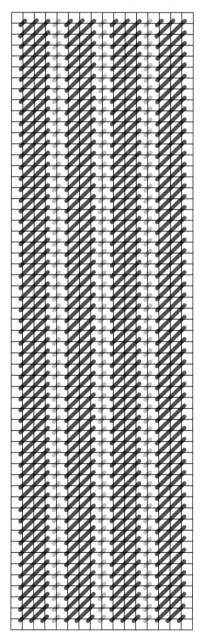

Doorstop Front/Back
(27 x 57 threads) (Work 2)

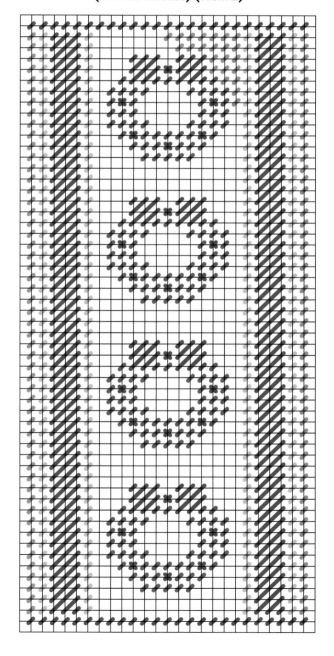

NL COLOR

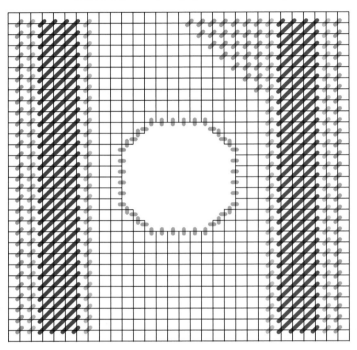

02 Christmas red

27 holly

41 white

metallic gold cord

Tissue Box Cover Top (31 x 31 threads)

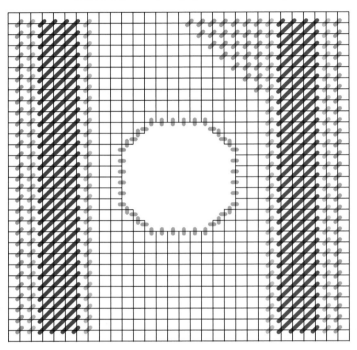

Tissue Box Cover Side (31 x 38 threads) (Work 4)

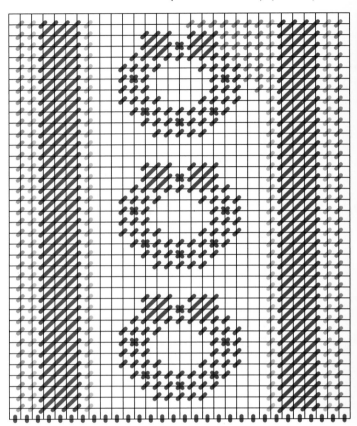

Mug Insert (65 x 24 threads)

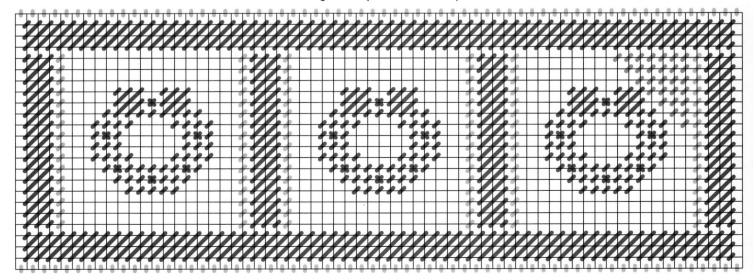

Jolly Santa Coasters

When you want to add a merry touch to your holiday gatherings, set your table with these jolly Santa coasters. They'll protect your tabletops and spread a little Christmas cheer. Santa Claus will be delighted while he enjoys his midnight snack, too!

SANTA COASTER

Skill Level: Beginner

Size: 3⅝"w x 5⅝"h

Supplies For Four Coasters: Worsted weight yarn or Needloft® Plastic Canvas Yarn (refer to color key), one 10½" x 13½" sheet of 7 mesh plastic canvas, #16 tapestry needle, cork or felt (optional), and clear-drying craft glue

Stitches Used: Backstitch, French Knot, Gobelin Stitch, Overcast Stitch, Tent Stitch, and Turkey Loop

Instructions: Follow chart and use required stitches to work Coaster. If backing is desired, cut cork or felt slightly smaller than Coaster and glue to wrong side of stitched piece.

Santa Coaster designed by Peggy Astle.

NL	COLOR		NL	COLOR
00	black - 1 yd		56	peach - 9 yds
02	red - 6 yds		02	red Fr. Knot
07	pink - 3 yds		41	white Fr. Knot
27	green - 1 yd		41	white Turkey Loop
41	white - 28 yds			

Coaster (30 x 30 threads) (Work 4)

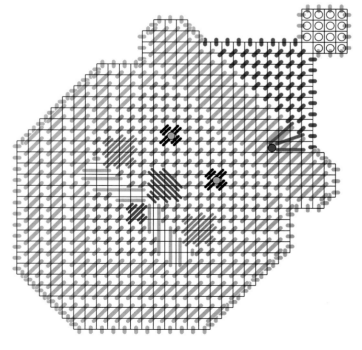

PEACE AND JOY

Displayed during the holiday season, this festive wall hanging will spread the message of peace on earth and goodwill toward men. Coordinating dove ornaments carry the joyous sentiment to the Christmas tree.

DOVE WALL HANGING & ORNAMENT

Skill Level: Intermediate
Wall Hanging Size: 13¾"w x 14½"h
Ornament Size: 4"w x 2⅞"h

Supplies: Worsted weight yarn or Needloft® Plastic Canvas Yarn (refer to color key), one 10½" x 13½" sheet of 7 mesh plastic canvas, one 10½" x 13½" sheet of 10 mesh plastic canvas, #16, #20, and #26 tapestry needles, 13" length of ⅜" dia wooden dowel (may be painted), two ⅝" dia wooden beads (may be painted), four 5" lengths of 1⅜"w plaid ribbon, 36" of ¼"w red satin ribbon, 36" of ¼"w green satin ribbon, 36" of ⅛"w green satin ribbon, 36" of ⅛"w red/white polka dot satin ribbon, 36" of ⅛"w white satin ribbon, artificial holly leaves, polyester fiberfill, nylon line, and clear-drying craft glue

Stitches Used: Alicia Lace, Alternating Mosaic Stitch, Backstitch, Cross Stitch, French Knot, Gobelin Stitch, Overcast Stitch, and Tent Stitch

Wall Hanging Instructions: Follow chart and use required stitches to work Base Top Section on 7 mesh plastic canvas. Follow chart and use required stitches to work Base Bottom Section below Base Top Section. Follow charts and use required stitches to work Leaves and Dove on 10 mesh plastic canvas. Use red Overcast Stitches to cover unworked edges of Base. Use white Overcast Stitches to cover unworked edges of Dove. Refer to photo to glue Dove and Leaves to Base. Refer to photo to glue ends of 1⅜"w ribbons to wrong side of stitched piece, forming loops. Thread dowel through loops. Glue wooden beads to dowel. Refer to photo to tie remaining ribbons in a bow and trim ends. Glue bow and artificial holly leaves to stitched piece.

Ornament Instructions: Follow chart and use required stitches to work Dove on 10 mesh plastic canvas. Cut out another Dove from 10 mesh plastic canvas. Turn Dove over (head should be on the left) and work with white Tent Stitches and a red Cross Stitch eye. With wrong sides together, use white to join Doves while lightly stuffing with polyester fiberfill. For hanger, thread 8" of nylon line through stitched piece. Tie ends together in a knot 3" above Ornament.

Dove Wall Hanging & Ornament designed by Jack Peatman for LuvLee Designs.

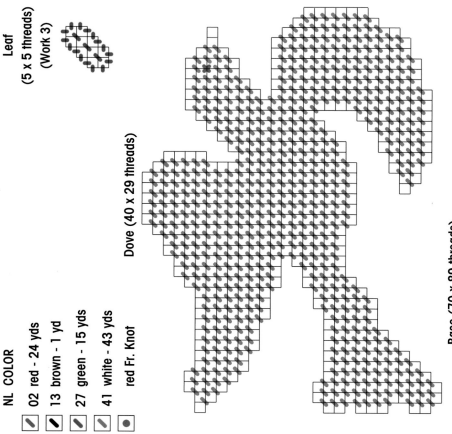

Leaf (5 x 5 threads) (Work 3)

Dove (40 x 29 threads)

NL	COLOR	
02	red - 24 yds	
13	brown - 1 yd	
27	green - 15 yds	
41	white - 43 yds	
	red Fr. Knot	

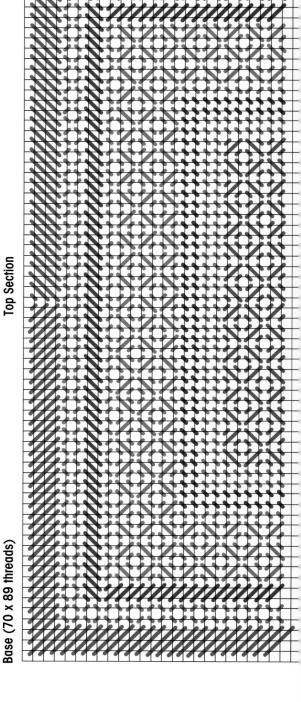

Top Section

Base (70 x 89 threads)

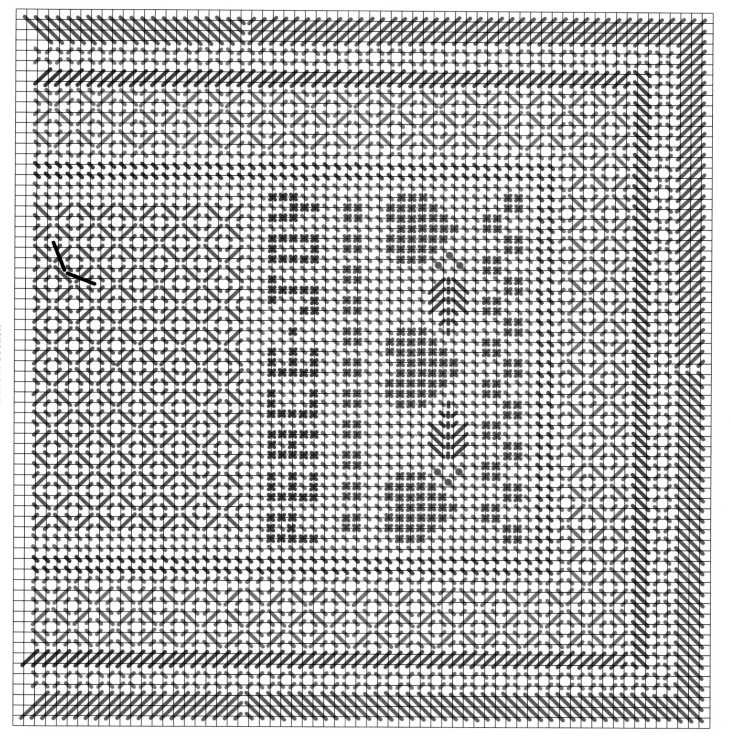

Candy Guard

*This toy soldier does double duty — not only
does he stand guard over your Yuletide festivities,
but his head lifts off to reveal a secret container.
What a fun place to store your holiday goodies!*

Tin Soldier Boy

TOY SOLDIER COFFEE CAN COVER

Skill Level: Intermediate

Size: 6½"w x 10"h x 6"d

Supplies: Needloft® Plastic Canvas Yarn or worsted weight yarn (refer to color keys), metallic gold cord, two 10½" x 13½" sheets of 7 mesh plastic canvas, two 4" dia plastic canvas circles, #16 tapestry needle, and 13 ounce coffee can with plastic lid (5½"h x 4" dia)

Stitches Used: Alicia Lace, Backstitch, Couching, Cross Stitch, French Knot, Gobelin Stitch, and Overcast Stitch

Instructions: Follow chart to cut Hat Brim from one 4" dia circle along pink cutting line. Follow charts and use required stitches to work Toy Soldier Coffee Can Cover pieces, leaving shaded areas and extended stitches unworked. (**Note:** Extended stitches on color charts have dots extending from them. They should be worked as long stitches across joined pieces of canvas.) Refer to photo for yarn color used for joining. For each Arm, refer to photo and match ★'s to join sections of Arm. Match ▲'s to join Hand to Arm. Match ✳'s to join Arm Top to Arm. Match ▼'s to join Arm, Arm Top, and Hand to Body, leaving area between ■'s unworked. Match ■'s to join Cuff and Arm to Body. Match ✦'s and work horizontal stitches in shaded area to join ends of Body, forming a cylinder. Work vertical stitches in shaded area to cover horizontal stitches. Work stitches with

dots extending from them. With wrong sides together, use metallic gold cord to join Key pieces. Use metallic gold cord and match ✪'s to join Key to Body. With wrong sides together, join Feet pieces, leaving area between ◆'s unworked. Match ◆'s to join Feet to Body. Match ÷'s and work horizontal stitches in shaded area to join ends of Neck, forming a cylinder. Work vertical stitches in shaded area to cover horizontal stitches. Join Neck to Neck Top, leaving areas between ✳'s unworked. For each Shoulder, refer to photo to join Fringe to Shoulder. Match ✳'s to join Shoulder and Fringe to Neck and Neck Top. Match ✧'s and work horizontal stitches in shaded area to join ends of Head, forming a cylinder. Work vertical stitches in shaded area to cover horizontal stitches. Refer to photo and match ◆'s to join sections of Head. Refer to photo to join Head to Neck Top. Match ÷'s and work horizontal stitches in shaded area to join ends of Hat, forming a cylinder. Work vertical stitches in shaded area to cover horizontal stitches. Refer to photo and match ☆'s to join sections of Hat. Match ✳'s to join Hat Brim to Hat. Refer to photo to join Chin Straps to Hat and Neck Top, securing Hat to Head. Place coffee can inside Body.

Toy Soldier Coffee Can Cover designed by Teresa S. Hannaway.

NL	COLOR	
✏	00	black - 14 yds
✏	02	Christmas red - 50 yds
✏	02	Christmas red - 2 strands
✏	32	royal - 49 yds
✏	32	royal - 2 strands
✏	39	eggshell - 18 yds
✏	39	eggshell - 2 strands
✏	41	white - 12 yds
✏	41	white - 2 strands
✏		metallic gold cord - 7 yds
●	39	eggshell Fr. Knot
⌣	00	black Couching

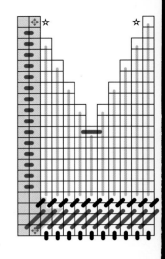

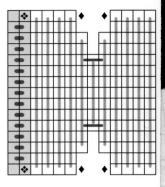

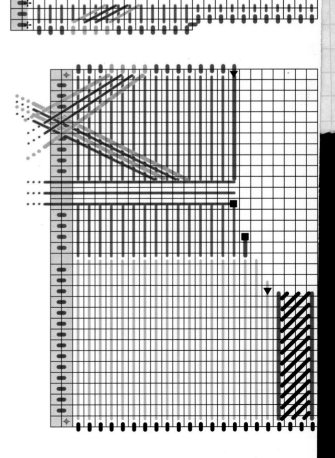

Hat (69 x 21 threads)

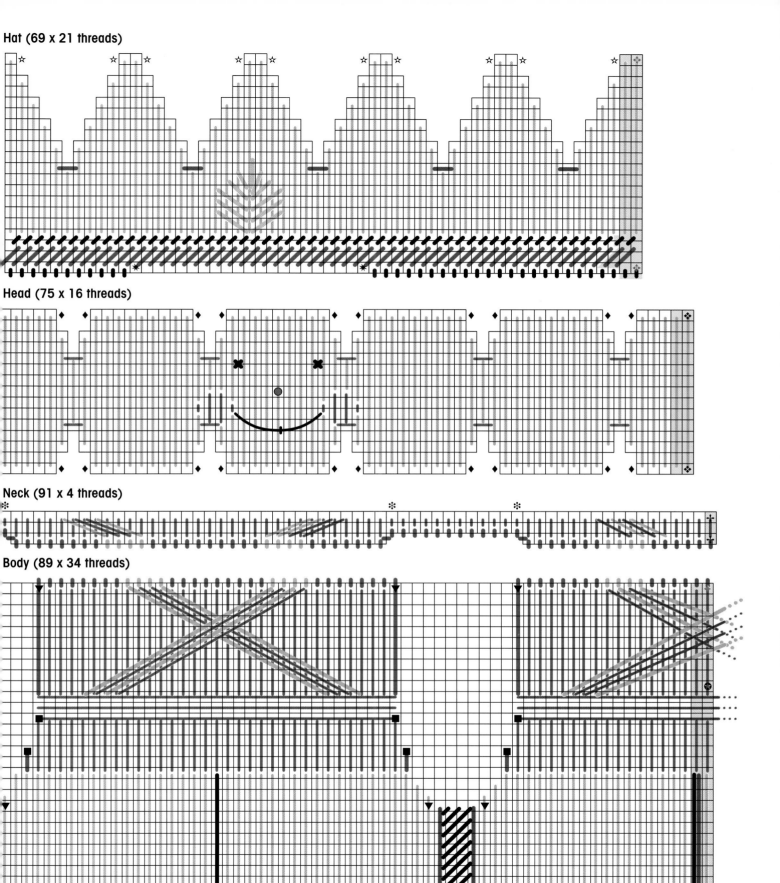

Head (75 x 16 threads)

Neck (91 x 4 threads)

Body (89 x 34 threads)

NL COLOR

	NL	COLOR
✎	00	black
✎	02	Christmas red
✎	02	Christmas red - 2 strands
✎	32	royal
✎	32	royal - 2 strands
✎	41	white
✎	41	white - 2 strands
✎		metallic gold cord

Hand
(5 x 3 threads)
(Work 2)

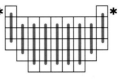

Shoulder
(12 x 8 threads) (Work 2)

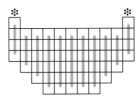

Arm Top
(10 x 7 threads) (Work 2)

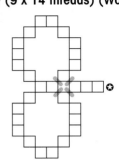

Arm (19 x 22 threads) (Work 2)

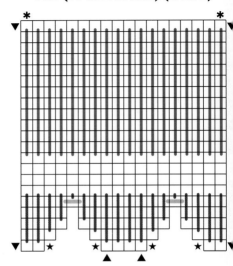

Chin Strap
(2 x 15 threads)
(Work 2)

Key (9 x 14 threads) (Work 2)

Cuff (21 x 5 threads) (Work 2)

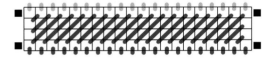

Feet (27 x 11 threads) (Work 2)

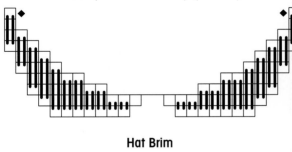

Fringe (22 x 4 threads) (Work 2)

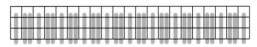

Neck Top

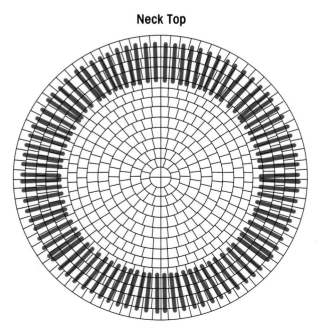

Hat Brim

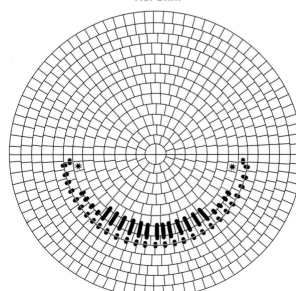

CHRISTMAS BUTTON COVERS

*Here's a quick way to bring holiday cheer to a plain shirt —
dress it up with our merry button covers! The festive accents
work up quickly on 10 mesh plastic canvas, so you'll have
plenty of time to make extra sets for gift-giving.*

SANTA AND PEPPERMINT BUTTON COVERS
Skill Level: Beginner
Santa Size: 1½"w x 1½"h
Peppermint Size: 1⅝"w x 1"h
Supplies: DMC embroidery floss (refer to color key), one 10½" x 13½" sheet of 10 mesh plastic canvas, #20 tapestry needle, sewing needle, and thread

Stitches Used: French Knot, Gobelin Stitch, Overcast Stitch, and Tent Stitch
Instructions: Use six strands of embroidery floss for French Knots and twelve strands for all other stitches. Follow charts and use required stitches to work Button Cover pieces. Use sewing thread to tack Back to wrong side of stitched piece.

*Santa and Peppermint Button Covers
designed by Becky Dill.*

DMC	COLOR	
◿	blanc	white - 15 yds
◿	666	red - 8 yds
◿	754	peach - 1 yd
●	311	blue Fr. Knot - 1 yd
●	666	red Fr. Knot

Back (11 x 9 threads)

Peppermint (17 x 10 threads)
(Work 4)

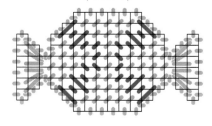

Santa (15 x 15 threads)

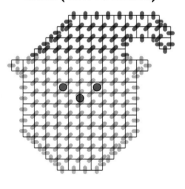

Frosty Fun

*This merry collection lets you capture the frosty fun of winter.
You can dress up a wreath with our cheery snowman and a flurry
of snowflakes, or trim the tree with snowman ornaments and a
sprinkling of the snowflakes. Either way, you'll have a jolly holiday!*

SNOWMAN WREATH

Skill Level: Intermediate
Size: 21" dia
Snowman Size: 8⅛"w x 10"h
5 Mesh Snowflake Size: 5½"w x 5½"h
7 Mesh Snowflake Size: 4¼"w x 4¼"h
10 Mesh Snowflake Size: 2¾"w x 2¾"h
Supplies: Worsted weight yarn or Needloft® Plastic Canvas Yarn (refer to color key), white sport weight yarn, one 13⅝" x 21⅝" sheet of 5 mesh plastic canvas, one 10½" x 13½" sheet of 7 mesh plastic canvas, one 10½" x 13½" sheet of 10 mesh plastic canvas, #13, #16, and #24 tapestry needles, two 12mm moving eyes, bead garland, 21" dia wreath, and clear-drying craft glue
Stitches Used: Backstitch, Double Cross Stitch Variation, Double Leviathan Stitch, French Knot, Overcast Stitch, and Tent Stitch
Instructions: Use two strands of worsted weight yarn on 5 mesh plastic canvas. Use sport weight yarn on 10 mesh plastic canvas. Follow charts and use required stitches to work Snowman, Hat Brim, Nose, Scarf pieces, Arms, Bird, Wing, and Snowflake on 5 mesh plastic canvas. Follow chart and use required stitches to work three Snowflakes on 7 mesh plastic canvas and three Snowflakes on 10 mesh plastic canvas. Refer to photo and use orange to tack Nose to Snowman. Refer to photo to glue Hat Brim and Scarf pieces to Snowman. Refer to photo to glue moving eyes to Snowman. Refer to photo to glue Arms to wrong side of Snowman. Glue Wing to Bird. Glue Bird to Snowman. Refer to photo to glue Snowman, Snowflakes, and bead garland to wreath.

SNOWMAN ORNAMENT

Skill Level: Beginner
Size: 3"w x 4⅞"h
Supplies: Worsted weight yarn or Needloft® Plastic Canvas Yarn (refer to color key), one 10½" x 13½" sheet of 7 mesh plastic canvas, #16 tapestry needle, 9mm moving eyes, nylon line, #26 tapestry needle (for working with nylon line), and clear-drying craft glue
Stitches Used: French Knot, Overcast Stitch, and Tent Stitch
Instructions: Follow charts and use required stitches to work Snowman Ornament, Hat Brim, Nose, and Scarf pieces. Refer to photo and use orange to tack Nose to Snowman Ornament. Refer to photo to glue Hat Brim and Scarf pieces to Snowman Ornament. Refer to photo to glue moving eyes to Snowman Ornament. For hanger, thread 8" of nylon line through stitched piece. Tie ends together in a knot 3" above Ornament.

SNOWFLAKE ORNAMENT

Skill Level: Beginner
Supplies: White worsted weight yarn or Needloft® Plastic Canvas Yarn, white sport weight yarn, one 10½" x 13½" sheet of 7 mesh plastic canvas, one 10½" x 13½" sheet of 10 mesh plastic canvas, #16 and #24 tapestry needles, and nylon line
Stitches Used: Backstitch, Double Leviathan Stitch, Overcast Stitch, and Tent Stitch
Instructions: Use sport weight yarn on 10 mesh plastic canvas. Follow chart and use required stitches to work Snowflake. For hanger, thread 8" of nylon line through stitched piece. Tie ends together in a knot 3" above Ornament.

Snowman and Snowflake Ornaments designed by Sandy and Honey for Studio M.

	NL	COLOR		NL	COLOR
✏	00	black	✏	41	white
✏	15	brown	✏	58	orange
✏	20	yellow	●	00	black Fr. Knot
✏	32	blue			

Snowman Ornament (17 x 23 threads)

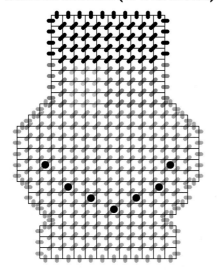

Snowflake (28 x 28 threads)

Hat Brim (20 x 3 threads)

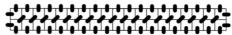

Nose (4 x 4 threads)

Snowman (23 x 50 threads)

Scarf A (15 x 5 threads)

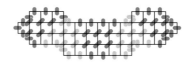

Scarf B (10 x 10 threads) (Work 2)

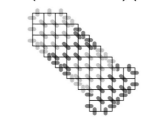

Arm (18 x 9 threads) (Work 2)

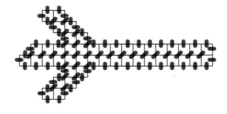

Bird (10 x 10 threads)

Wing (5 x 5 threads)

CANDLE COLLECTION

Brighten your holiday with this illuminating collection! It offers an assortment of dazzling projects, including a tissue box cover, a Christmas card holder, a star-shaped coaster, and an elegant trinket box. You'll even find decorative accents for your holiday candles!

CANDLE SET

Skill Level: Intermediate

Supplies For Entire Set: Worsted weight yarn or Needloft® Plastic Canvas Yarn (refer to color keys), Kreinik heavy (#32) metallic gold braid, one 10½" x 13½" sheet of clear 7 mesh plastic canvas, seven 10½" x 13½" sheets of white 7 mesh plastic canvas, #16 tapestry needle, 98 - 3mm gold beads, cork or felt, nylon line, beading needle, and clear-drying craft glue

Stitches Used: Backstitch, Cross Stitch, French Knot, Gobelin Stitch, Overcast Stitch, and Tent Stitch

CANDLE BAND

Size: 2¼"w x 1½"h

Instructions: Cut Candle Band from clear plastic canvas. Follow chart and use required stitches to work Candle Band. Use nylon line to sew one bead to Candle Band at each ★. Use metallic gold braid and match ▲'s to join ends of Candle Band along unworked edges.

CANDLE RING

Size: 3¼"w x 3¼"h

Instructions: Cut Candle Ring from white plastic canvas. Follow chart and use required stitches to work Candle Ring. Use nylon line to sew one bead to Candle Ring at each ★.

CARD HOLDER

Size: 10"w x 8½"h x 5"d

Instructions: Cut Holly pieces from clear plastic canvas. Cut remaining Card Holder pieces from white plastic canvas. Follow charts and use required stitches to work Card Holder pieces. Use nylon line to sew one bead to Front at each ★. Use blue for all joining. With wrong sides together, match ▲'s to join Sides to Front. Refer to photo and match ◆'s to join Back to Sides. Match ♥'s to join Bottom to Front, Back, and Sides. Match *'s to glue Holly pieces to Front and Back.

TRINKET BOX

Size: 5⅝"w x 6¼"h x 5⅝"d

Instructions: Cut Inner Band, Outer Band, Holly Front, and Holly Back from clear plastic canvas. Cut remaining Trinket Box pieces from white plastic canvas. Follow charts and use required stitches to work Trinket Box pieces, leaving stitches in shaded areas unworked. Use nylon line to sew one bead to Candle Front, Candle Back, and Top at each ★. With right side facing in, match ♥'s to join short ends of Inner Band, forming a ring. Match ♥'s to fit Inner Band inside Outer Band. Use metallic gold braid to join Inner Band to Outer Band along unworked edges between ■'s and ▶'s. Refer to photo and match ◆'s to join ends of Outer Band along unworked edges. Refer to photo and use metallic gold braid to tack Band to Top. With wrong sides together, work stitches in shaded areas to join Candle Front to Candle Back. Match ♣'s to place Candle Sides on Candle Front and Back. Work stitches in shaded areas to join Candle Sides to Candle Front and Back through four thicknesses. Use metallic gold braid to join Candle Front and Candle Back to Top between ▲'s. Refer to photo and use green to tack Holly Front to Holly Back. Use green to tack Holly to Candle and Band. For Top Sides, cut four pieces of white plastic canvas 4 x 24 threads each. Use blue to join Top Sides along short edges. Work stitches in shaded areas to join Top Sides to wrong side of Top. For Bottom, cut a piece of white plastic canvas 27 x 27 threads. Use blue to join Bottom Sides along short edges. Use blue to join Bottom Sides to Bottom along second thread from outer edge of Bottom.

COASTER

Size: 4¾"w x 4¾"h

Instructions: Cut Coaster from white plastic canvas. Follow chart and use required stitches to work Coaster. For backing, cut cork or felt slightly smaller than Coaster and glue to wrong side of stitched piece.

TISSUE BOX COVER

Size: 4⅞"w x 6¾"h x 4⅞"d

(**Note:** Fits a 4¼"w x 5¼"h x 4¼"d boutique tissue box.)

Instructions: Cut Leaf and Holly pieces from clear plastic canvas. Cut remaining Tissue Box Cover pieces from white plastic canvas. Follow charts and use required stitches to work Tissue Box Cover pieces. Use nylon line to sew one bead to Top and Sides at each ★. Use blue for all joining. Join Sides along long edges. Refer to photo to join Top to Sides. Refer to photo and match ▲'s to glue Holly to Sides. Refer to photo and match ◆'s to glue Leaves to Sides.

Candle Set designed by Dick Martin.

NL	COLOR
00	black - 4 yds
02	red - 58 yds
27	green - 23 yds
32	blue - 216 yds
	metallic gold braid - 99 yds
02	red Fr. Knot

Coaster (32 x 32 threads)

**Candle Ring
(22 x 22 threads)**

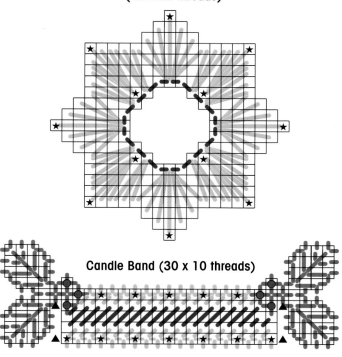

Candle Band (30 x 10 threads)

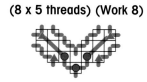

Tissue Box Cover Side (32 x 45 threads) (Work 4)

**Tissue Box Cover Leaf
(4 x 4 threads) (Work 8)**

**Tissue Box Cover Holly
(8 x 5 threads) (Work 8)**

Tissue Box Cover Top (32 x 32 threads)

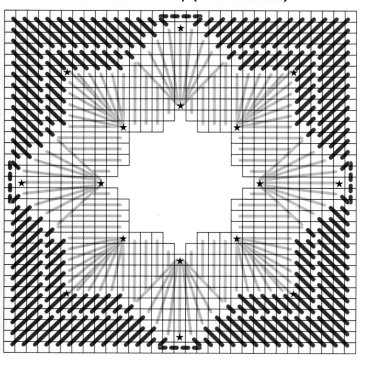

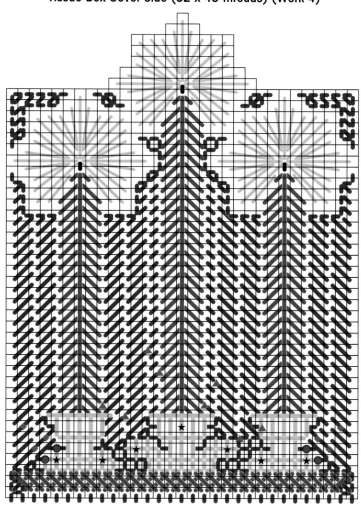

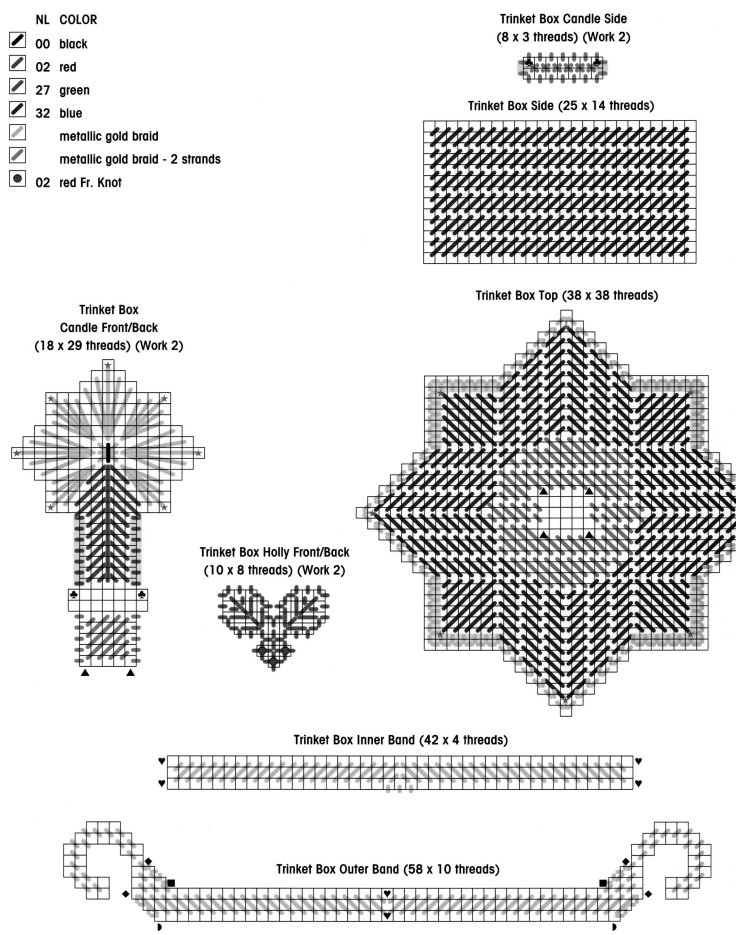

NL COLOR

	00	black
	02	red
	27	green
	32	blue
		metallic gold braid
		metallic gold braid - 2 strands
	02	red Fr. Knot

Trinket Box Candle Side
(8 x 3 threads) (Work 2)

Trinket Box Side (25 x 14 threads)

Trinket Box Top (38 x 38 threads)

Trinket Box
Candle Front/Back
(18 x 29 threads) (Work 2)

Trinket Box Holly Front/Back
(10 x 8 threads) (Work 2)

Trinket Box Inner Band (42 x 4 threads)

Trinket Box Outer Band (58 x 10 threads)

Card Holder Bottom (66 x 33 threads)

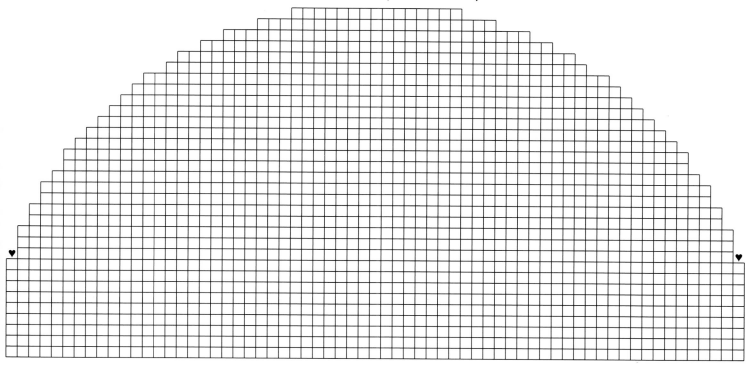

Card Holder Front (66 x 35 threads)

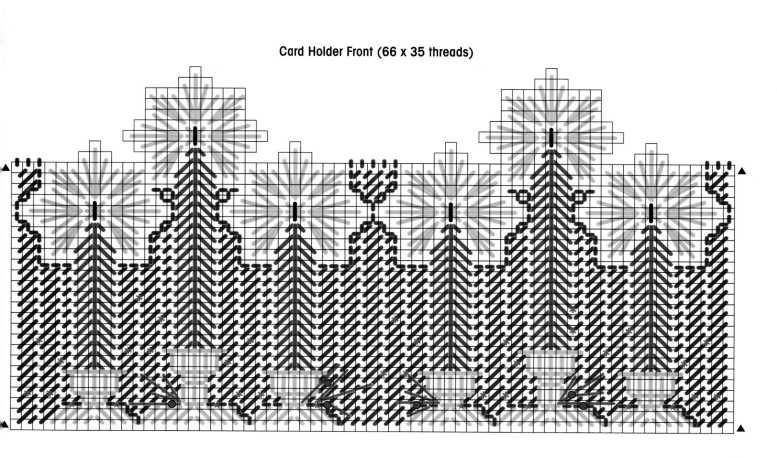

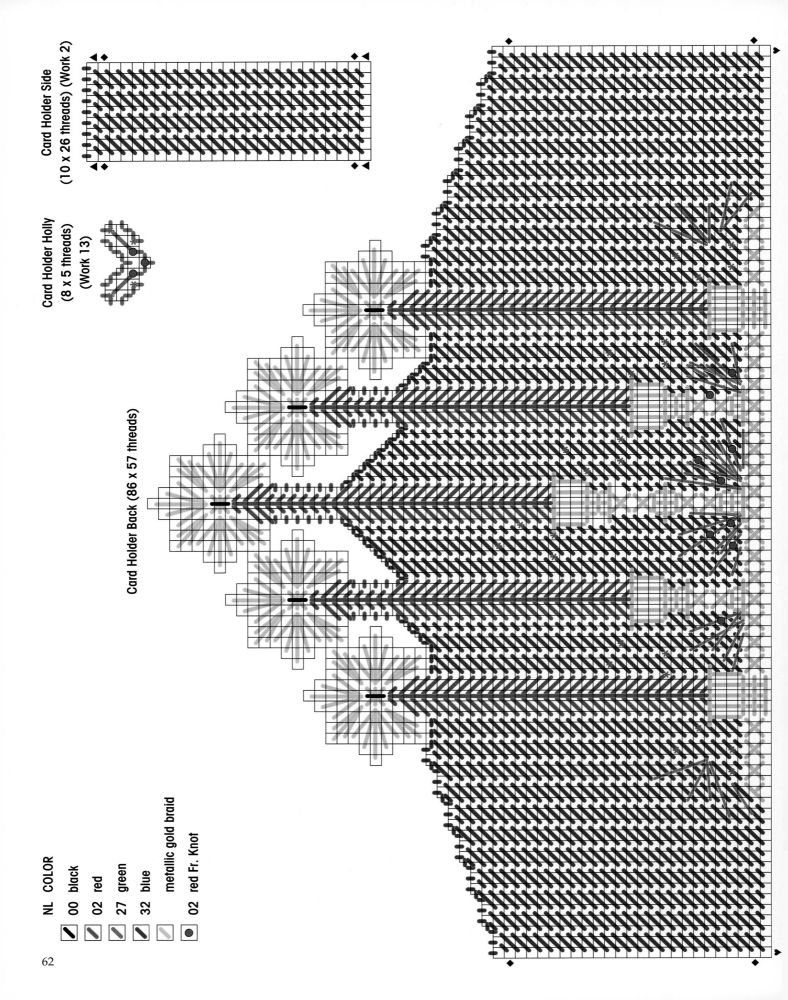

Card Holder Side
(10 x 26 threads) (Work 2)

Card Holder Holly
(8 x 5 threads)
(Work 13)

Card Holder Back (86 x 57 threads)

NL COLOR
00 black
02 red
27 green
32 blue
     metallic gold braid
02 red Fr. Knot

Snowman Stocking Holder

With his wintry smile and outstretched arms, this cheery snowman will be happy to hold your Christmas stocking. Worked on 7 mesh canvas, he'll keep a steady hand even when the stocking is filled with holiday treats — his back is as strong as a brick!

SNOWMAN STOCKING HOLDER

Skill Level: Beginner

Size: 6½"w x 9⅞"h x 6⅜"d

Supplies: Worsted weight yarn or Needloft® Plastic Canvas Yarn (refer to color key), six-strand embroidery floss (refer to color key), two 10½" x 13½" sheets of 7 mesh plastic canvas, #16 tapestry needle, 3⅝"w x 8½"h x 2¾"d brick, plastic wrap, nylon line, and #26 tapestry needle (for working with nylon line)

Stitches Used: Backstitch, French Knot, Fringe, Gobelin Stitch, Overcast Stitch, Tent Stitch, and Upright Cross Stitch

Instructions: Follow charts and use required stitches to work Snowman Stocking Holder pieces. Use yarn color to match stitching area to join Arm A to Arm B along unworked edges, leaving areas between symbols open. Use white and match ▲'s to join Arm A to Snowman. Use white and match ★'s to join Arm B to Snowman. Use white to join Long Sides to Short Sides along short edges. Use white to join Front to Sides. Refer to photo and use nylon line to securely tack Snowman to Front. Wrap brick with plastic wrap and insert brick. Use white to join Back to Sides.

Snowman Stocking Holder designed by Debbie Tabor.

Short Side (28 x 18 threads) (Work 2)

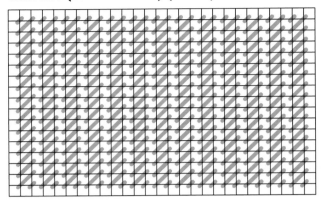

Long Side (56 x 18 threads) (Work 2)

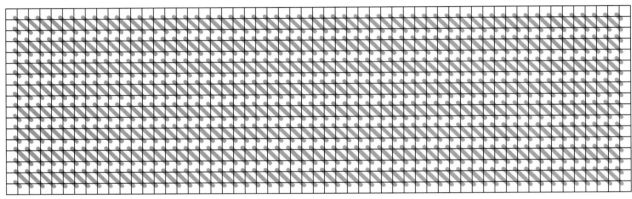

Front/Back (56 x 28 threads) (Work 2)

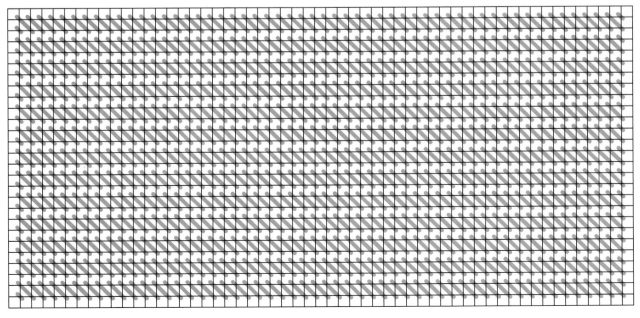

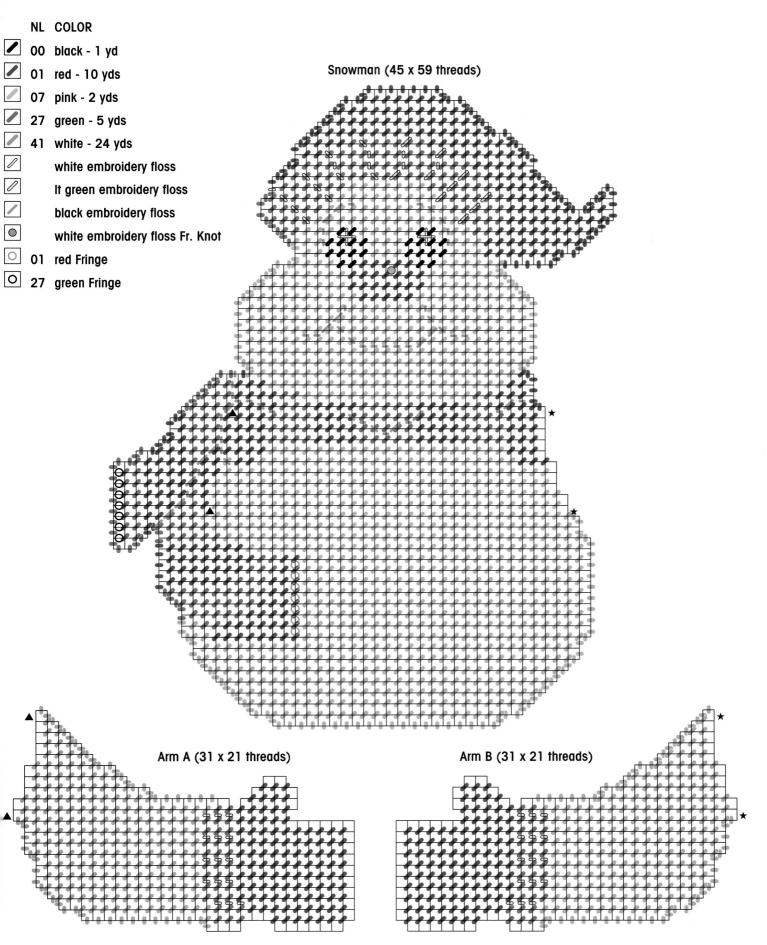

NL COLOR

00 black - 1 yd
01 red - 10 yds
07 pink - 2 yds
27 green - 5 yds
41 white - 24 yds
white embroidery floss
lt green embroidery floss
black embroidery floss
white embroidery floss Fr. Knot
01 red Fringe
27 green Fringe

Snowman (45 x 59 threads)

Arm A (31 x 21 threads)

Arm B (31 x 21 threads)

Stained-Glass Inspirations

Reminiscent of stained glass windows, these elegant ornaments are stitched on 14 mesh plastic canvas. They get their brilliant color from glass seed beads and metallic ribbon.

STAINED-GLASS ORNAMENTS
Skill Level: Intermediate
Size: 1⅞"w x 1⅞"h each
Supplies: One 8" x 11" sheet of 14 mesh plastic canvas, #10 crewel needle, #24 tapestry needle, Kreinik ¹/₁₆"w metallic ribbon (refer to color key), Mill Hill Glass Seed Beads (refer to color key), nylon line, and white quilting thread
Stitches Used: Beaded Tent Stitch, Gobelin Stitch, Overcast Stitch, and Tent Stitch
Instructions: Follow chart and use required stitches to work Ornament. Use quilting thread and crewel needle to work Beaded Tent Stitches. For hanger, thread 8" of nylon line through stitched piece. Tie ends together in a knot 3" above Ornament.

Stained-Glass Ornaments designed by Carol Krob.

	KREINIK	COLOR		BEAD	COLOR
✎	002HL	gold	✎	167	Christmas green
✎	005HL	black	✎	252	iris
✎	007HL	pink	✎	2009	ice lilac
✎	014HL	sky blue	✎	2011	victorian gold
✎	015	chartreuse	✎	2012	royal plum

Ornament #1 (27 x 27 threads)

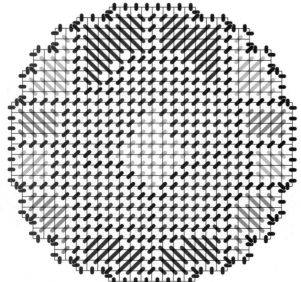

Ornament #2 (27 x 27 threads)

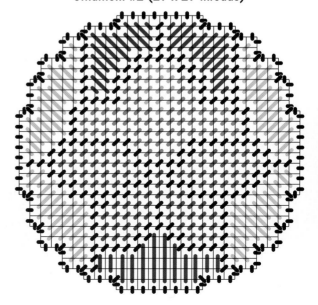

SANTA BEAR STOCKING

*An adorable Santa bear peeks over the cuff of this keepsake stocking,
which makes a wonderful Christmas gift. Stuffed with tiny treasures
and sweet treats, the roomy stocking will delight children of all ages!*

TEDDY STOCKING

Skill Level: Intermediate

Size: 11 1/8"w x 15 1/2"h

Supplies: Worsted weight yarn or Needloft® Plastic Canvas Yarn (refer to color key), two 12" x 18" sheets of 7 mesh plastic canvas, #16 tapestry needle, 6" of 5/8"w red satin ribbon, sewing needle, and thread

Stitches Used: Alternating Scotch Stitch, Overcast Stitch, and Tent Stitch

Instructions: Follow chart and use required stitches to work Stocking Front in center of one sheet of plastic canvas, omitting Overcast Stitches. Use chart as guide to cut out Stocking Front, leaving one unworked thread around entire stitched area. Use Stocking Front as pattern to cut out Stocking Back. Work charted Overcast Stitches on Stocking Front. Turn Stocking Back over (toe should be on the left). Work Stocking Back with red Alternating Scotch Stitches over four threads. With wrong sides together, use yarn color to match stitching area to join Stocking Front to Stocking Back along unworked edges of Stocking Front. Work red Overcast Stitches to cover unworked edge of Stocking Back. For hanger, refer to photo to tack ribbon to wrong side of Stocking Back.

Teddy Stocking designed by Kooler Design Studio, Inc.

NL	COLOR	
00	black - 3 yds	
01	lt red - 7 yds	
02	red - 135 yds	
13	lt brown - 6 yds	
14	brown - 3 yds	

NL	COLOR	
17	gold - 4 yds	
19	lt gold - 6 yds	
23	lt green - 19 yds	
27	dk green - 3 yds	

NL	COLOR	
28	green - 10 yds	
37	grey - 4 yds	
39	ecru - 5 yds	
41	white - 17 yds	

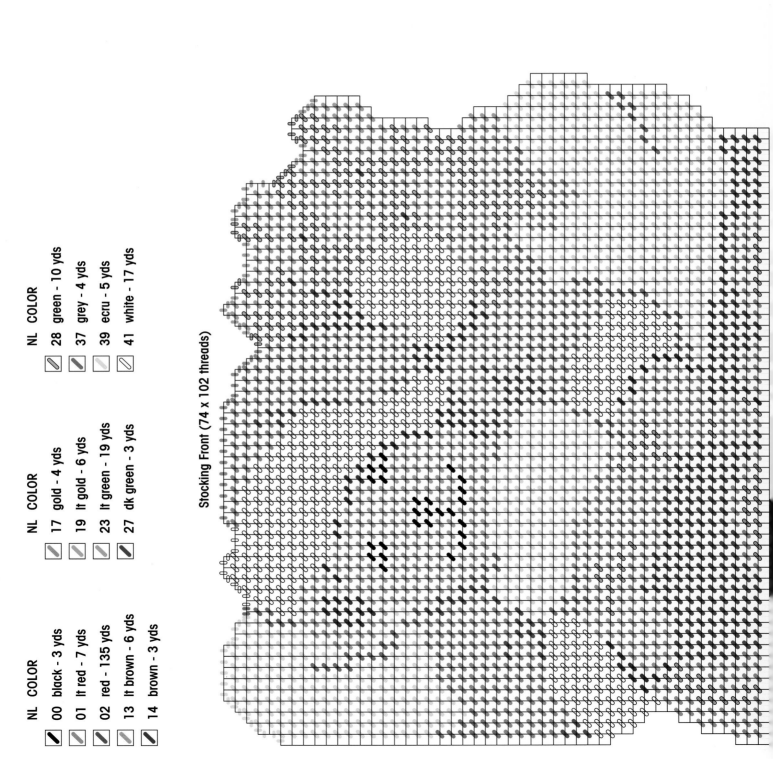

Stocking Front (74 x 102 threads)

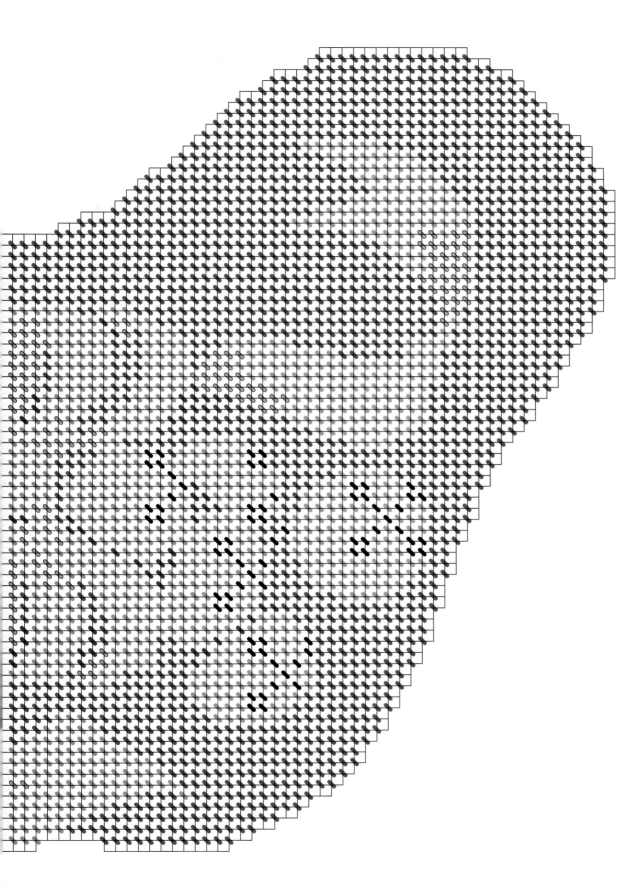

Nostalgic Card Holder

Carolers rejoice beneath the warm glow of a streetlamp on this nostalgic holder, which is perfect for storing greeting cards from loved ones. Colorful bead "ornaments" grace the wintry evergreens, and an electric candle hidden in the lamppost illuminates the scene.

CAROLER CARD HOLDER

Skill Level: Intermediate

Size: 8¼"w x 12¼"h x 4¾"d

Supplies: Worsted weight yarn or Needloft® Plastic Canvas Yarn (refer to color keys), three 10½" x 13½" sheets of 7 mesh plastic canvas, #16 tapestry needle, 5"h x ⅞" dia electric candle, red (#05025) and gold (#05557) Mill Hill Glass Pebble Beads, sewing needle and thread, and clear-drying craft glue or hot glue gun and glue sticks

Stitches Used: Alicia Lace, Backstitch, Cross Stitch, French Knot, Fringe, Gobelin Stitch, Mosaic Stitch, Overcast Stitch, Tent Stitch, and Turkey Loop

Instructions: Follow charts and use required stitches to work Caroler Card Holder pieces, using a double thickness of canvas for Front, Back, and Sides. Use sewing needle and thread to attach beads to Carolers. Use white to join Front and Back to Sides. For Bottom, cut a piece of plastic canvas 51 x 21 threads. (**Note:** Bottom is not worked.) Use white to join Bottom to Front, Back, and Sides. Refer to photo to glue Carolers to Front. Use green for remainder of joining. Refer to Diagram and match like symbols to assemble Post Top and two Post Side pieces. Join Post Sides and Post Top pieces to Post Front. Join remaining Post Side to assembled Post Sides along long edges. Use green Overcast Stitches to cover unworked edges of Post Top pieces and Post Side. Refer to photo to glue Post to Back. Insert electric candle in Post.

Caroler Card Holder designed by Jack Peatman for LuvLee Designs.

Diagram

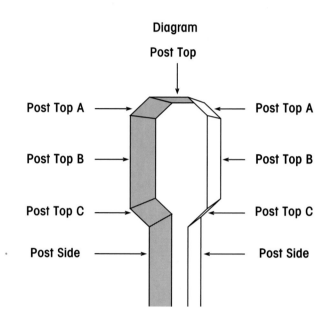

Front/Back (51 x 30 threads) (Work 2)

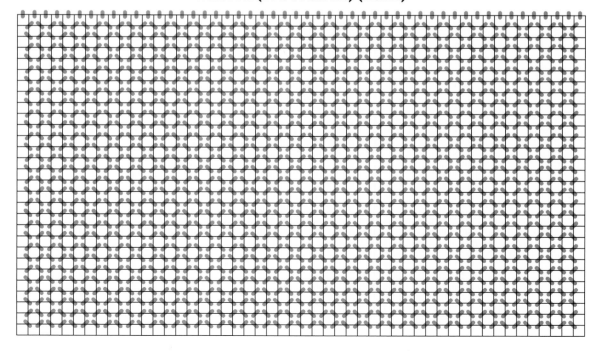

NL	COLOR		NL	COLOR		NL	COLOR
00	black - 1 yd		28	green - 30 yds			grey 2-ply - 1 yd
00	black 2-ply		29	dk green - 3 yds			gold beads
01	red - 13 yds			dk green 2-ply			red beads
	red 2-ply		32	blue - 2 yds		01	red Fr. Knot
07	pink - 1 yd			blue 2-ply		01	red Fringe
13	brown - 1 yd		35	lt blue - 3 yds		16	lt brown Turkey Loop
16	lt brown - 7 yds		41	white - 68 yds			
19	yellow - 10 yds		56	flesh - 2 yds			

Carolers (55 x 57 threads)

NL COLOR

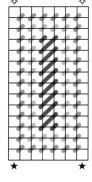

- 01 red
- 19 yellow
- 28 green
- 41 white

Post Top B
(8 x 15 threads)
(Work 2)

Post Top (8 x 8 threads)

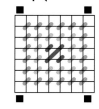

Post Top C
(8 x 4 threads)
(Work 2)

Post Top A
(8 x 5 threads)
(Work 2)

Side (21 x 30 threads) (Work 2)

Post Side
(8 x 61 threads)
(Work 3)

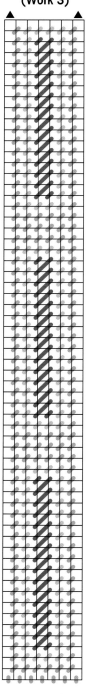

Post Front (14 x 81 threads)

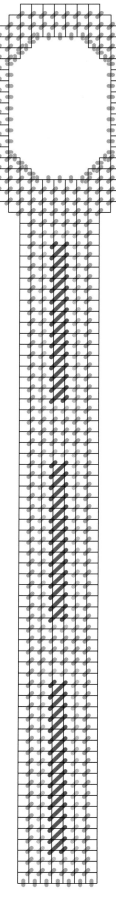

Fanciful Santas

Elegant trimmings give these Santa ornaments their fanciful beards. Fashioned from 7 mesh plastic canvas, the ornaments both take shape from the same easy pattern and are given individual appeal with pearl or lace accents on their beards. Metallic thread adds sparkle to their caps, which are embellished with fuzzy pom-poms.

SANTA ORNAMENTS
Skill Level: Beginner
Size: 2⅝"w x 3½"h each
Supplies: Worsted weight yarn or Needloft® Plastic Canvas Yarn (refer to color key), metallic yarn (refer to color key), one 10½" x 13½" sheet of 7 mesh plastic canvas, #16 tapestry needle, nylon line, two 1" white pom-poms, sixty 4mm white pearls, 18" of ⅜"w pre-gathered white lace, beading needle, thread, and clear-drying craft glue
Stitches Used: Backstitch, French Knot, Gobelin Stitch, Overcast Stitch, and Tent Stitch
Instructions: Follow chart and use required stitches to work Santa Ornament. Refer to photo to glue pom-pom to Ornament. For hanger, thread 8" of nylon line through stitched piece. Tie ends together in a knot 3" above Ornament. **For Ornament with pearls only:** Refer to photo and use beading needle and thread to sew pearls to Ornament. **For Ornament with lace only:** Beginning at the bottom edge, refer to photo to cut and glue rows of lace to Ornament.

Santa Ornaments designed by Joan Green.

NL	COLOR
07	pink - 1 yd
41	white - 3 yds
56	flesh - 1 yd
	metallic red - 1 yd
	metallic black - 1 yd
	metallic red Fr. Knot

Santa Ornament (19 x 24 threads)

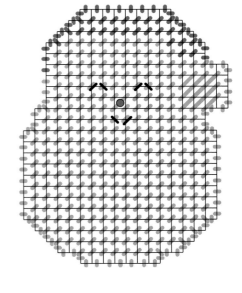

Gifts From The Kitchen

Whip up some merry little gifts from the kitchen with this quick-to-make collection, which includes a pair of holiday bags for delivering your homemade treats. You'll also find Yuletide designs for topping jars of candy and package clips for spreading holiday cheer.

GIFT BAGS

Skill Level: Beginner

Approx Size: 5¾"w x 7¼"h x 2⅝"d each

Supplies: Worsted weight yarn or Needloft® Plastic Canvas Yarn (refer to color key), two 10½" x 13½" sheets of white 7 mesh plastic canvas, two 10½" x 13½" sheets of Christmas green 7 mesh plastic canvas, #16 tapestry needle, three 5mm red pom-poms, and clear-drying craft glue

Stitches Used: Alternating Overcast Stitch, Backstitch, French Knot, Overcast Stitch, and Tent Stitch

Instructions: Refer to photo for design placement. Follow chart and use required stitches to work desired Motif on Front. Use red and white Alternating Overcast Stitches for all joining. Join Front and Back to Sides along long edges. For Bottom, cut a piece of plastic canvas 39 x 18 threads. (**Note:** Bottom is not worked.) Join Bottom to Front, Back, and Sides. Use red and white Alternating Overcast Stitches to cover unworked edges. For each handle, cut nine 24" lengths of yarn. Tie yarn lengths together 2" from one end. Thread long loose yarn ends through right side of Front at ▲. Refer to photo to braid yarn to desired handle length. Thread ends of yarn through wrong side of Front at ♦. Knot yarn on right side of Front and trim ends. Repeat for remaining handle on Back. **For Stocking Motif only,** follow charts and use required stitches to work Gift Bag Stocking Top, Gift Bag Berry, and two Gift Bag Leaves. Refer to photo to glue Leaves and Berry to Stocking Top. Glue Stocking Top to Front. **For Candle Motif only,** follow chart and use required stitches to work five Gift Bag Leaves. Refer to photo to glue Leaves and pom-poms to Front.

BAG CLIPS

Skill Level: Beginner

Approx Size: 2½"w x 3"h each

Supplies: Worsted weight yarn or Needloft® Plastic Canvas Yarn (refer to color key), one 10½" x 13½" sheet of 7 mesh plastic canvas, #16 tapestry needle, clothespin, and clear-drying craft glue

Stitches Used: French Knot, Overcast Stitch, and Tent Stitch

Instructions: Follow charts and use required stitches to work Bag Clip pieces. Glue clothespin to wrong side of completed Bag Clip. **For Mitten only,** refer to photo to glue Heart to Mitten. **For Joy only,** refer to photo to glue letters to Joy. **For Heart only,** refer to photo to glue Leaves and Berries to Heart.

JAR LIDS

Skill Level: Beginner

Approx Size: 3⅛"w x 3⅛"h each

Supplies: Worsted weight yarn or sport weight yarn (refer to color key), one 10½" x 13½" sheet of 10 mesh plastic canvas, #20 tapestry needle, large-mouth jar lid ring, three 5mm yellow pom-poms, and clear-drying craft glue

Stitches Used: Overcast Stitch and Tent Stitch

Instructions: Follow charts and use required stitches to work Jar Lid pieces. Glue Jar Lid Top into jar lid ring. **For Poinsettia only,** refer to photo to glue Large Petals and Small Petals to Top. Glue pom-poms to Small Petals. **For Holly only,** refer to photo to glue Leaves and Berries to Top.

Bag Clips, Gift Bags, and Jar Lids designed by Sandy and Honey for Studio M.

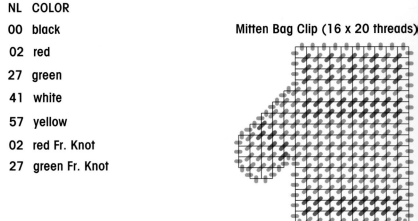

NL	COLOR
✏	00 black
✏	02 red
✏	27 green
✏	41 white
✏	57 yellow
●	02 red Fr. Knot
●	27 green Fr. Knot

Mitten Bag Clip (16 x 20 threads)

Mitten Bag Clip Heart (6 x 6 threads)

Joy Bag Clip (8 x 20 threads)

"J" (5 x 6 threads)

"O" (5 x 6 threads)

"Y" (6 x 6 threads)

Heart Bag Clip (20 x 17 threads)

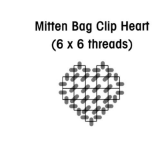

Heart Bag Clip Berry (4 x 4 threads) (Work 3)

Heart Bag Clip Leaf (7 x 7 threads) (Work 2)

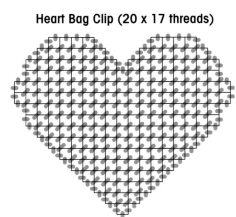

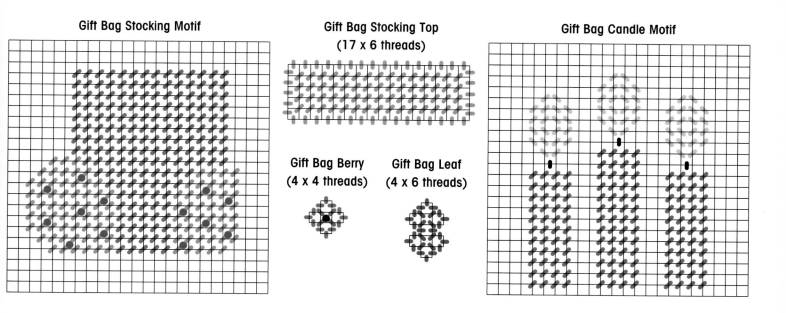

Gift Bag Stocking Motif

Gift Bag Stocking Top
(17 x 6 threads)

Gift Bag Candle Motif

Gift Bag Berry
(4 x 4 threads)

Gift Bag Leaf
(4 x 6 threads)

Gift Bag Front/Back (39 x 49 threads) (Cut 2)

Gift Bag Side
(18 x 49 threads) (Cut 2)

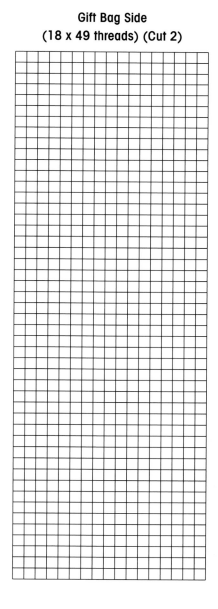

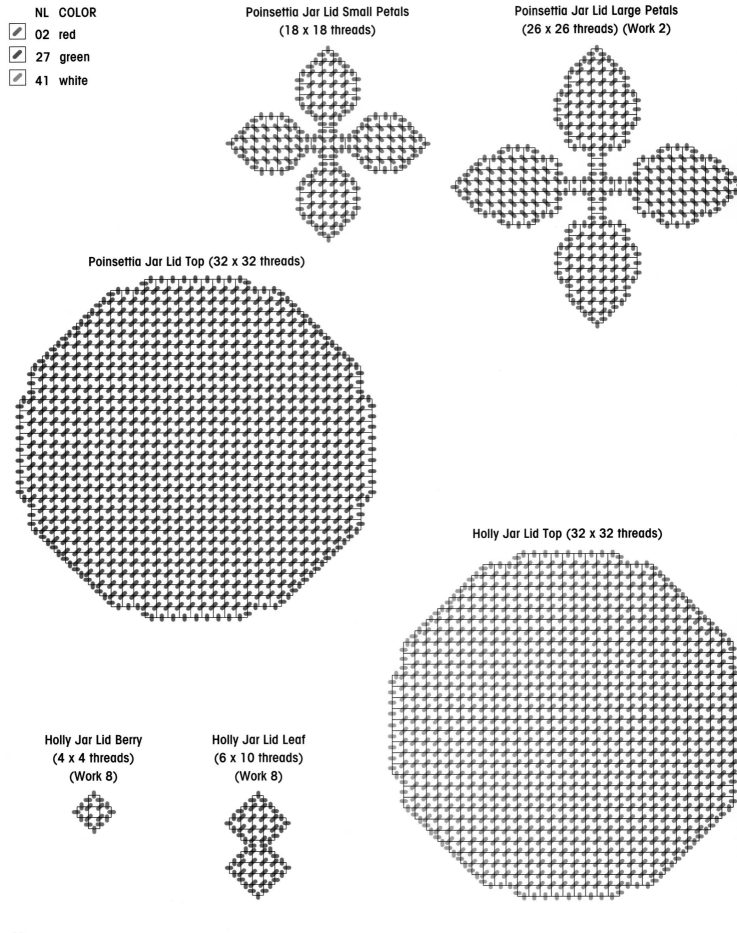

NL COLOR

02 red

27 green

41 white

Poinsettia Jar Lid Small Petals
(18 x 18 threads)

Poinsettia Jar Lid Large Petals
(26 x 26 threads) (Work 2)

Poinsettia Jar Lid Top (32 x 32 threads)

Holly Jar Lid Top (32 x 32 threads)

Holly Jar Lid Berry
(4 x 4 threads)
(Work 8)

Holly Jar Lid Leaf
(6 x 10 threads)
(Work 8)

O Holy Night

This tissue box cover elegantly displays the Nativity scene. Fashioned in blue and white for a striking nighttime look, the cover is studded with brilliant gold bead "stars." Metallic gold cord makes the Star of Bethlehem shine, and a musical button lets you celebrate the joy of the Savior's birth with a familiar carol.

MUSICAL NATIVITY TISSUE BOX COVER

Skill Level: Intermediate

Size: 4³/₄"w x 7"h x 4³/₄"d

(**Note:** Fits a 4¹/₄"w x 5¹/₄"h x 4¹/₄"d boutique tissue box.)

Supplies: Worsted weight yarn or Needloft® Plastic Canvas Yarn (refer to color key), two 10¹/₂" x 13¹/₂" sheets of clear 7 mesh plastic canvas, two 10¹/₂" x 13¹/₂" sheets of white 7 mesh plastic canvas, metallic gold cord, #16 tapestry needle, 143 - 3mm gold round beads, two 12mm gold sequins, one 8mm gold sequin, nylon line, #26 tapestry needle (for working with nylon line), music button, and clear-drying craft glue

Stitches Used: Backstitch, Gobelin Stitch, Overcast Stitch, and Tent Stitch

Instructions: Cut Nativity, Trees, and Staff from white plastic canvas. Cut remaining pieces from clear plastic canvas. Follow charts and use required stitches to work Musical Nativity Tissue Box Cover pieces. Use nylon line to sew beads to pieces. Refer to photo to glue sequins to wrong side of Nativity. Refer to photo and use nylon line to tack Trees, Staff, and Nativity to Sides. Use blue for all joining. With right sides together, match ■'s to join Backs to Base. With right sides facing inward, join Inner Sides along short edges. Match ▲'s to join Inner Sides to wrong side of Top. With right sides facing outward, join Outer Sides along short edges. Match ◆'s to join Outer Sides to Base. Glue music button to Base at ◆. Placing music button under gold star on Top, join Top to Outer Sides. Join Inner Sides to Base. Join Sides to Base and Backs. Join Sides along unworked edges.

Musical Nativity Tissue Box Cover designed by Dick Martin.

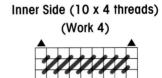

NL	COLOR	
/	32	blue - 130 yds
/	41	white - 14 yds
/		metallic gold cord - 5 yds
●		bead placement

Inner Side (10 x 4 threads)
(Work 4)

Outer Side (26 x 4 threads) (Work 4)

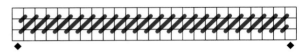

Side (32 x 47 threads) (Work 4)

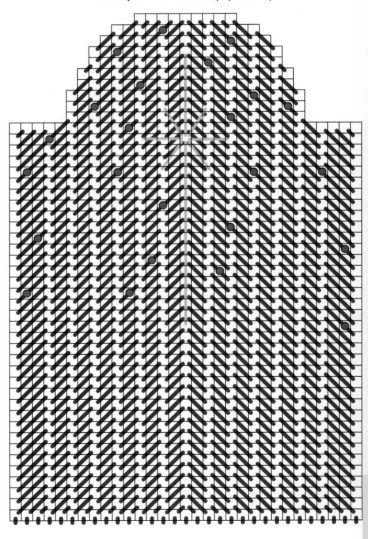

Base (32 x 32 threads)

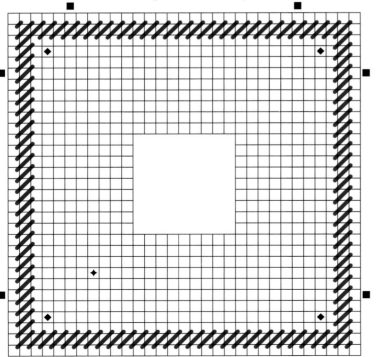

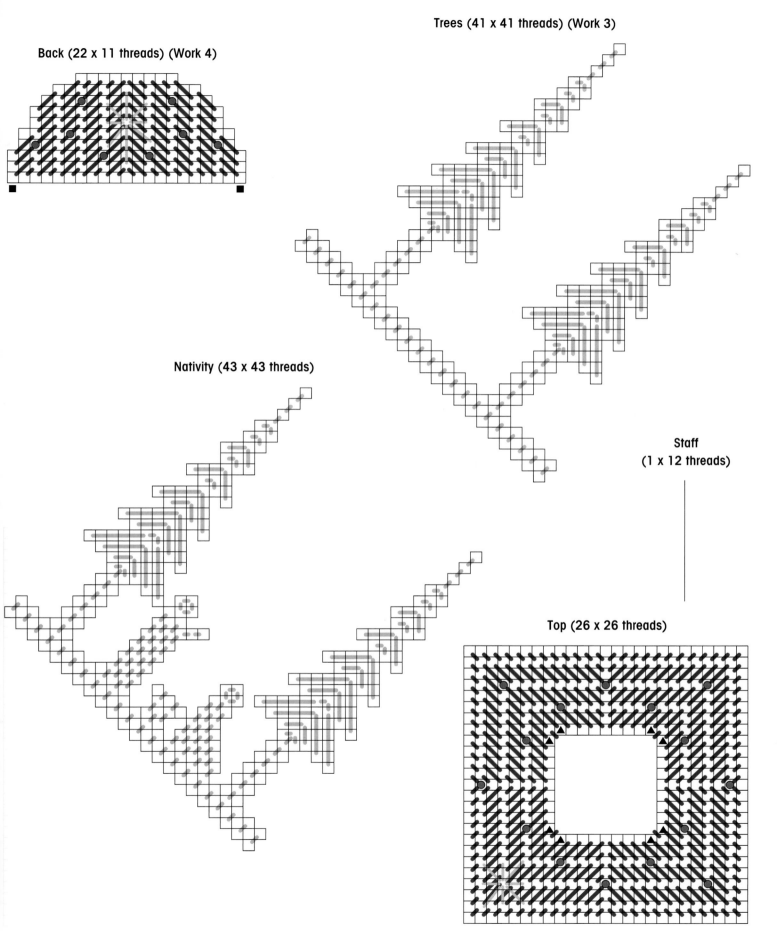

Back (22 x 11 threads) (Work 4)

Trees (41 x 41 threads) (Work 3)

Nativity (43 x 43 threads)

**Staff
(1 x 12 threads)**

Top (26 x 26 threads)

83

Holiday Sparkle

The merry motifs in this collection are sure to add sparkle to the holidays. Stitched on 7 mesh canvas, the ten designs offer a bright way to add Christmas cheer to a wreath. The set can also be stitched on 14 mesh canvas and made into fun fashion accessories.

ORNAMENTS

Skill Level: Beginner
Approx Size: 4¾"w x 4¼"h each
Supplies: Worsted weight yarn or Needloft® Plastic Canvas Yarn (refer to color keys), Kreinik medium (#16) gold braid, two 10½" x 13½" sheets of 7 mesh plastic canvas, #16 tapestry needle, 8" of 1/16"w red satin ribbon, nylon line, #26 tapestry needle (for working with nylon line), and clear-drying craft glue
Stitches Used: Backstitch, Cross Stitch, French Knot, Gobelin Stitch, Mosaic Stitch, Overcast Stitch, Scotch Stitch, and Tent Stitch

Instructions: Follow charts and use required stitches to work Ornament pieces. (**Note:** Use two strands of metallic braid for good coverage.) For hanger, thread an 8" length of nylon line through stitched piece. Tie ends together in a knot 3" above Ornament. **For Angel only,** cut a 2" length of metallic gold braid and fold in half. Refer to photo to glue folded end of braid to wrong side of Angel and loose ends to wrong side of Heart. **For Bell only,** refer to photo to glue Large Leaves to Bell. **For Candy Cane only,** refer to photo to thread an 8" length of green yarn through stitched piece. Tie yarn in a bow and trim ends. **For Gingerbread House only,** tie ribbon in a bow and trim ends. Glue bow to Wreath. Refer to photo to glue Wreath to Gingerbread House. **For Star only,** refer to photo and use green to tack Leaves to Star. **For Santa only,** refer to photo to glue Small Leaves to Santa.

Ornaments designed by Dick Martin.

JEWELRY

Skill Level: Intermediate
Necklace Size: 21" long
Earring Size: ½"w x ¾"h
Approx Lapel Pin Size: 2"w x 2¼"h each
Supplies: DMC embroidery floss (refer to color keys), Kreinik medium (#16) gold braid, two 8" x 11" sheets of 14 mesh plastic canvas, #24 tapestry needle, 1" long pin back, two 4mm flat post earring backs, five 5mm jump rings, gold clasp, assorted beads (refer to photo), 48" of 1/16"w red satin ribbon, 1 yard of waxed dental floss, needle nose pliers, and clear-drying craft glue
Stitches Used: Backstitch, Cross Stitch, French Knot, Gobelin Stitch, Mosaic Stitch, Overcast Stitch, Scotch Stitch, and Tent Stitch

Earring Instructions: Follow charts and use required stitches to work two Large Leaves, using six strands of embroidery floss. Glue flat posts to wrong sides of stitched pieces.
Lapel Pin Instructions: Follow charts and use required stitches to work desired pieces, using six strands of embroidery floss. Follow Ornament Instructions to assemble pieces. Glue pin back to wrong side of Ornament.

Necklace Instructions: Follow charts and use required stitches to work all Ornament pieces, using six strands of embroidery floss. Follow Ornament Instructions to assemble pieces. Tie one end of dental floss to clasp. Refer to photo to string beads onto dental floss. Tie remaining end of dental floss to remaining clasp. Refer to photo to thread 3" of ribbon through top of Angel. To secure, fold one end of ribbon ¼" over Angel and glue in place on back of ribbon. Wrap remaining end of ribbon around center of beaded string. Fold ribbon ¼" over dental floss and glue in place on back of ribbon. Use needle nose pliers to place one jump ring each through top of Bell, Tree, Gingerbread House, Candle, and Star. Refer to photo to attach Gingerbread House to center of beaded string. Refer to photo to attach remaining Ornaments with jump rings to beaded string approximately 2" apart. Refer to photo to wrap 3" of ribbon around necklace halfway between two Ornaments. Thread loose ends of ribbon through top of Candy Cane. Glue ends of ribbon to wrong side of stitched piece. Repeat for Horse, Santa, and Train. Tie a 6" length of ribbon in a bow around each ribbon loop close to beaded string.

NL	DMC	COLOR		NL	DMC	COLOR
✎ 00	410	black	◻		blanc	white 2-ply
✎ 02	666	red	◻	47	353	peach
◻ 07	894	pink	◻			metallic gold
✎ 13	781	brown	●	00	410	black Fr. Knot
◻ 18	738	tan	◉	02	666	red Fr. Knot
✎ 28	909	green	◉	07	894	pink Fr. Knot
◻ 41	blanc	white	◉			metallic gold Fr. Knot

Train (32 x 25 threads)

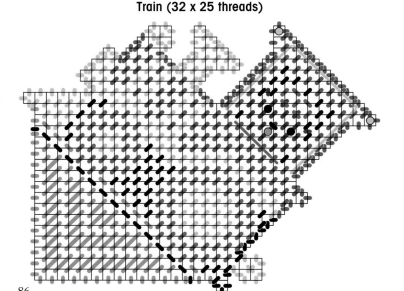

Tree (25 x 25 threads)

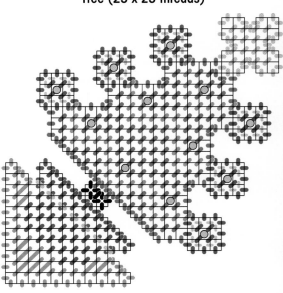

Heart
(5 x 5 threads)

Small Leaves
(8 x 5 threads)

Angel (25 x 25 threads)

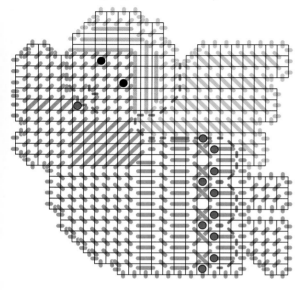

Santa (28 x 25 threads)

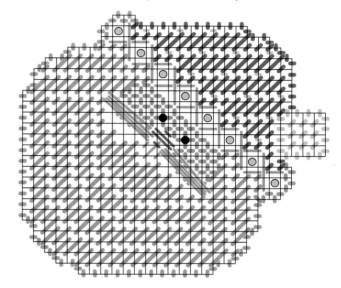

Wreath
(5 x 5 threads)

Leaf
(6 x 6 threads)
(Work 4)

Gingerbread House (28 x 28 threads)

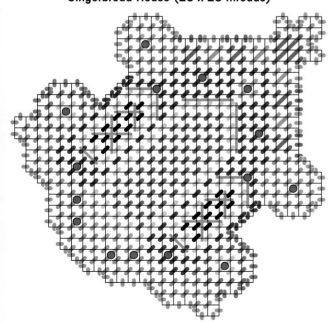

Star (27 x 27 threads)

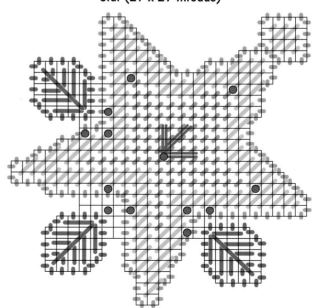

NL	DMC	COLOR
00	410	black
02	666	red
07	894	pink
13	781	brown
18	738	tan
28	909	green

NL	DMC	COLOR
41	blanc	white
		metallic gold
00	410	black Fr. Knot
02	666	red Fr. Knot
28	909	green Fr. Knot
		metallic gold Fr. Knot

Large Leaves
(10 x 8 threads)
(Work 2)

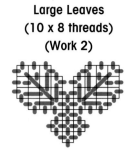

Candy Cane (25 x 27 threads)

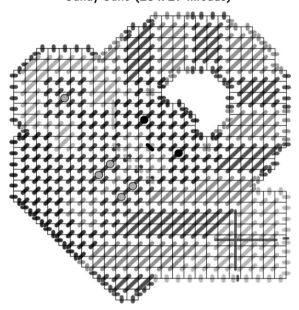

Bell (25 x 25 threads)

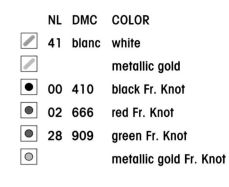

Horse (28 x 29 threads)

Candle (26 x 26 threads)

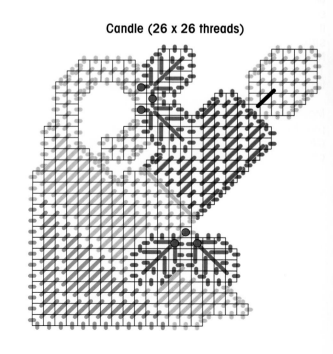

GENERAL INSTRUCTIONS
SELECTING PLASTIC CANVAS

Plastic canvas is a molded, nonwoven canvas made from clear or colored plastic. The canvas consists of "threads" and "holes." The threads aren't actually "threads" since the canvas is nonwoven, but it seems to be an accurate description of the straight lines of the canvas. The holes, as you would expect, are the spaces between the threads. The threads are often referred to in the project instructions, especially when cutting out plastic canvas pieces. The instructions for stitches will always refer to holes when explaining where to place your needle to make a stitch.

TYPES OF CANVAS

The main difference between types of plastic canvas is the mesh size. Mesh size refers to the number of holes in one inch of canvas. The most common mesh sizes are 5 mesh, 7 mesh, 10 mesh, and 14 mesh. Five mesh means that there are 5 holes in every inch of canvas. Likewise, there are 7 holes in every inch of 7 mesh canvas, 10 holes in every inch of 10 mesh canvas, and 14 holes in every inch of 14 mesh canvas. Seven mesh canvas is the most popular size for projects.

Your project supply list will tell you what size mesh you need to buy. Be sure to use the mesh size the project instructions recommend. If your project calls for 7 mesh canvas and you use 10 mesh, your finished project will be much smaller than expected. For example, say your instructions tell you to use 7 mesh canvas to make a boutique tissue box cover. You will need to cut each side 30 x 38 threads so they will measure 4½" x 5¾" each. But if you were using 10 mesh canvas your sides would only measure 3" x 3⅞"! Needless to say, your tissue box cover from 10 mesh canvas would not fit a boutique tissue box.

Most plastic canvas is made from clear plastic, but colored canvas is also available. Colored plastic is ideal when you don't want to stitch the entire background.

When buying canvas, you may find that some canvas is firm and rigid, while other canvas is softer and more pliable. To decide which type of canvas is right for your project, think of how the project will be used. If you are making a box or container, you will want to use firmer canvas so that the box will be sturdy and not buckle after handling. If you are making a tissue box cover, you will not need the firmer canvas because the tissue box will support the canvas and prevent warping. Softer canvas is better for projects that require a piece of canvas to be bent before it is joined to another piece.

AMOUNT OF CANVAS

The project supply list usually tells you how much canvas you will need to complete the project. When buying your canvas, remember that several different manufacturers produce plastic canvas. Therefore, there are often slight variations in canvas, such as different thicknesses of threads or a small difference in mesh size. Because of these variations, try to buy enough canvas for your entire project at the same time and place. As a general rule, it is always better to buy too much canvas and have leftovers than to run out of canvas before you finish your project. By buying a little extra canvas, you not only allow for mistakes, but have extra canvas for practicing your stitches. Scraps of canvas are also excellent for making magnets and other small projects.

SELECTING YARN

You're probably thinking, "How do I select my yarn from the thousands of choices available?" Well, we have a few hints to help you choose the perfect yarns for your project and your budget.

TYPES OF YARN

The first question to ask when choosing yarn is, "How will my project be used?" If your finished project will be handled or used a lot, such as a coaster or magnet, you will want to use a durable, washable yarn. We highly recommend acrylic or nylon yarn for plastic canvas. It can be washed repeatedly and holds up well to frequent usage and handling. If your finished project won't be handled or used frequently, such as a framed picture or a bookend, you are not limited to washable yarns.

Cost may also be a factor in your yarn selection. There again, acrylic yarn is a favorite because it is reasonably priced and comes in a wide variety of colors. However, if your project is something extra special, you may want to spend a little more on tapestry yarn or Persian wool yarn to get certain shades of color.

The types of yarns available are endless, and each grouping of yarn has its own characteristics and uses. The following is a brief description of some common yarns used for plastic canvas.

Worsted Weight Yarn - This yarn may be found in acrylic, wool, wool blends, and a variety of other fiber contents. Worsted weight yarn is the most popular yarn used for 7 mesh plastic canvas because one strand covers the canvas very well. This yarn is inexpensive and comes in a wide range of colors. Worsted weight yarn has four plies which are twisted together to form one strand. When the instructions call for "2-ply" yarn, you will need to separate a strand of yarn into its four plies and use only the number of plies indicated in the instructions. Worsted weight yarn is used for most of the projects in this leaflet.

Needloft® Plastic Canvas Yarn - This yarn is 100% nylon and is especially designed to be used on 7 mesh plastic canvas. There are sixty-five colors from which to choose. Needloft® Yarn will not easily separate. When the instructions call for "2-ply" yarn, we recommend that you substitute with six strands of embroidery floss.

Sport Weight Yarn - This yarn has four thin plies which are twisted together to form one strand. Like worsted weight yarn, sport weight yarn comes in a variety of fiber contents. The color selection in sport weight yarn is more limited than in other types of yarns. You may want to use a double strand of sport weight yarn for better coverage of your 7 mesh canvas. When you plan on doubling your yarn, remember to double the yardage called for in the instructions, too. Sport weight yarn works nicely for 10 mesh canvas.

Tapestry Yarn - This is a thin wool yarn. Because tapestry yarn is available in a wider variety of colors than other yarns, it may be used when several shades of the same color are desired. For example, if you need five shades of pink to stitch a flower, you may choose tapestry yarn for a better blending of colors. Tapestry yarn is ideal for working on 10 mesh canvas. However, it is a more expensive yarn and requires two strands to cover 7 mesh canvas. Projects made with tapestry yarn cannot be washed.

Persian Wool - This is a wool yarn which is made up of three loosely twisted plies. The plies should be separated and realigned before you thread your needle. Like tapestry yarn, Persian yarn has more shades of each color from which to choose. It also has a nap similar to the nap of velvet. To determine the direction of the nap, run the yarn through your fingers. When you rub "with the nap," the yarn is smooth; but when you rub "against the nap," the yarn is rough. For smoother and prettier stitches on your project, stitching should be done "with the nap." The yarn fibers will stand out when stitching is done "against the nap." Because of the wool content, you cannot wash projects made with Persian yarn.

Pearl Cotton - Sometimes #3 pearl cotton is used on plastic canvas to give it a dressy, lacy look. It is not meant to cover 7 mesh canvas completely but to enhance it. Pearl cotton works well on 10 mesh canvas when you want your needlework to have a satiny sheen. If you cannot locate #3 pearl cotton in your area, you can substitute with twelve strands of embroidery floss.

Embroidery Floss - Occasionally, embroidery floss is used to add small details such as eyes or mouths on 7 mesh canvas. Twelve strands of embroidery floss are recommended for covering 10 mesh canvas. Use six strands to cover 14 mesh canvas.

COLORS

Choosing colors can be fun, but sometimes a little difficult. Your project will tell you what yarn colors you will need. When you begin searching for the recommended colors, you may be slightly overwhelmed by the different shades of each color. Here are a few guidelines to consider when choosing your colors.

Consider where you are going to place the finished project. If the project is going in a particular room in your house, match your yarn to the room's colors.

Try not to mix very bright colors with dull colors. For example, if you're stitching a project using country colors, don't use a bright Christmas red with country blues and greens. Instead, use a maroon or country red. Likewise, if you are stitching a bright tissue box cover for a child's room, don't use country blue with bright red, yellow, and green.

Some projects require several shades of a color, such as shades of red for a Santa. Be sure your shades blend well together.

Sometimes, you may have trouble finding three or four shades of a color. If you think your project warrants the extra expense, you can usually find several shades of a color available in tapestry yarn or Persian wool yarn.

Remember, you don't have to use the colors suggested in the color key. If you find a blue tissue box cover that you really like, but your house is decorated in pink, change the colors in the tissue box cover to pink!

AMOUNTS

A handy way of estimating yardage is to make a yarn yardage estimator. Cut a one yard piece of yarn for each different stitch used in your project. For each stitch, work as many stitches as you can with the one yard length of yarn.

To use your yarn yardage estimator, count the number of stitches you were able to make, say 72 Tent Stitches. Now look at the chart for the project you want to make. Estimate the number of ecru Tent Stitches on the chart, say 150. Now divide the estimated number of ecru stitches by the actual number stitched with a yard of yarn. One hundred fifty divided by 72 is approximately two. So you will need about two yards of ecru yarn to make your project. Repeat this for all stitches and yarn colors. To allow for repairs and practice stitches, purchase extra yardage of each color. If you have yarn left over, remember that scraps of yarn are perfect for small projects such as magnets or when you need just a few inches of a particular color for another project.

In addition to purchasing an adequate amount of each color of yarn, it is also important to buy all of the yarn you need to complete your project at the same time. Yarn often varies in the amount of dye used to color the yarn. Although the variation may be slight when yarns from two different dye lots are held together, the variation is usually very apparent on a stitched piece.

SELECTING NEEDLES
TYPES OF NEEDLES

Stitching on plastic canvas should be done with a blunt needle called a tapestry needle. Tapestry needles are sized by numbers; the higher the number, the smaller the needle. The correct size needle to use depends on the canvas mesh size and the yarn thickness. The needle should be small enough to allow the threaded needle to pass through the canvas holes easily, without disturbing canvas threads. The eye of the needle should be large enough to allow yarn to be threaded easily. If the eye is too small, the yarn will wear thin and may break. You will find the recommended needle size listed in the supply section of each project.

WORKING WITH PLASTIC CANVAS

Throughout this leaflet, the lines of the canvas will be referred to as threads. However, they are not actually "threads" since the canvas is nonwoven. To cut plastic canvas pieces accurately, count **threads** (not **holes**) as shown in **Fig. 1**.

Fig. 1

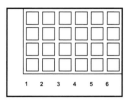

PREPARING AND CUTTING CANVAS

Before cutting out your pieces, notice the thread count of each piece on your chart. The thread count is usually located above the piece on the chart. The thread count tells you the number of threads in the width and the height of the canvas piece. Follow the thread count to cut out a rectangle the specified size. Remember to count **threads**, not **holes**. If you accidentally count holes, your piece is going to be the wrong size. Follow the chart to trim the rectangle into the desired shape.

You may want to mark the outline of the piece on your canvas before cutting it out. Use a China marker, grease pencil, or fine point permanent marker to draw the outline of your shape on the canvas. Before you begin stitching, be sure to remove all markings with a dry tissue. Any remaining markings are likely to rub off on your yarn as you stitch.

A good pair of household scissors is recommended for cutting plastic canvas. However, a craft knife is helpful when cutting a small area from the center of a larger piece of canvas. For example, a craft knife is recommended for cutting the opening out of a tissue box cover top. When using a craft knife, be sure to protect the table below your canvas. A layer of cardboard or a magazine should provide enough padding to protect your table.

When cutting canvas, be sure to cut as close to the thread as possible without cutting into the thread. If you don't cut close enough, "nubs" or "pickets" will be left on the edge of your canvas. Be sure to cut off all nubs from the canvas before you begin to stitch, because nubs will snag the yarn and are difficult to cover.

When cutting plastic canvas along a diagonal, cut through the center of each intersection. This will leave enough plastic canvas on both sides of the cut so that both pieces of canvas may be used. Diagonal corners will also snag yarn less and be easier to cover.

The charts may show slits in the plastic canvas **(Fig. 2)**. To make slits, use a craft knife to cut exactly through the center of an intersection of plastic canvas threads **(Fig. 3)**. Repeat for number of intersections needed. When working piece, be careful not to carry yarn across slits.

Fig. 2

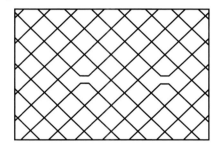

Fig. 3

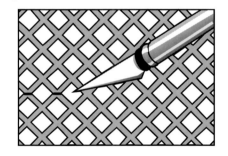

If your project has several pieces, you may want to cut them all out before you begin stitching. Keep your cut pieces in a sealable plastic bag to prevent loss.

THREADING YOUR NEEDLE

Many people wonder, "What is the best way to thread my needle?" Here are a couple of methods. Practice each one with a scrap of yarn and see what works best for you. There are also several yarn-size needle threaders available at your local craft store.

FOLD METHOD

First, sharply fold the end of yarn over your needle; then remove needle. Keeping the fold sharp, push the needle onto the yarn **(Fig. 4)**.

Fig. 4

THREAD METHOD

Fold a 5" piece of sewing thread in half, forming a loop. Insert loop of thread through the eye of your needle **(Fig. 5)**. Insert yarn through the loop and pull the thread back through your needle, pulling yarn through at the same time.

Fig. 5

WASHING INSTRUCTIONS

If you used washable yarn for all of your stitches, you may hand wash plastic canvas projects in warm water with a mild soap. Do not rub or scrub stitches; this will cause the yarn to fuzz. Allow your stitched piece to air dry. Do not put stitched pieces in a clothes dryer. The plastic canvas could melt in the heat of a dryer. Do not dry clean your plastic canvas. The chemicals used in dry cleaning could dissolve the plastic canvas. When piece is dry, you may need to trim the fuzz from your project with a small pair of sharp scissors.

GENERAL INFORMATION

1. **Fig. 1, page 91**, shows how to count threads accurately. Follow charts to cut out plastic canvas pieces.

2. To help you select colors for your projects, we have included numbers for Needloft® Plastic Canvas Yarn or Paternayan® Persian Yarn in some of our color keys. The headings in the color keys are for Needloft® Yarn (**NL**), Paternayan® Persian Yarn (**PTN**), and the descriptive color name (**COLOR**).

3. Backstitches used for detail **(Fig. 11)** and French Knots **(Fig. 20)** are worked over completed stitches.

4. Unless otherwise indicated, Overcast Stitches **(Fig. 24, page 94)** are used to cover edges of pieces and to join pieces.

STITCH DIAGRAMS

> Unless otherwise indicated, bring threaded needle up at 1 and all odd numbers and down at 2 and all even numbers.

ALICIA LACE

This series of stitches is worked in diagonal rows and forms a lacy pattern. Follow **Fig. 6** and work in one direction to cover every other diagonal row of intersections. Then work in the other direction **(Fig. 7)** to cover the remaining intersections.

Fig. 6

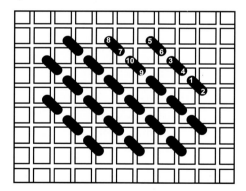

Fig. 7

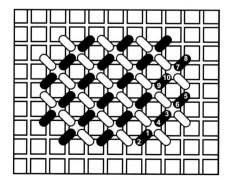

ALTERNATING MOSAIC STITCH

This three-stitch pattern forms small alternating squares as shown in **Fig. 8**.

Fig. 8

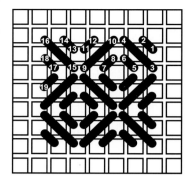

ALTERNATING OVERCAST STITCH

This stitch covers the edge of the canvas and joins pieces of canvas. With first color, work Overcast Stitches in every other hole. Then with second color, work Overcast Stitches in the remaining holes **(Fig. 9)**.

Fig. 9

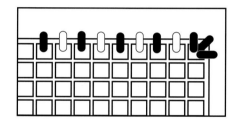

ALTERNATING SCOTCH STITCH

This Scotch Stitch variation is worked over three or more threads, forming alternating squares **(Fig. 10)**.

Fig. 10

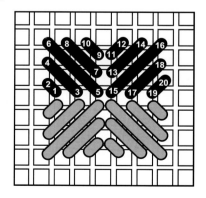

BACKSTITCH

This stitch is worked over completed stitches to outline or define **(Fig. 11)**. It is sometimes worked over more than one thread. Backstitch may also be used to cover canvas as shown in **Fig. 12**.

Fig. 11

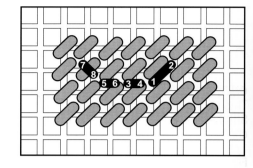

Fig. 12

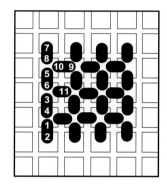

BEADED TENT STITCH

This stitch is simply a Tent Stitch with a bead slipped on the needle each time before going down at even numbers as shown in **Fig. 13**. Notice that your floss will slant up to the right just like on the chart but the beads will slant in the opposite direction (up to the left).

Fig. 13

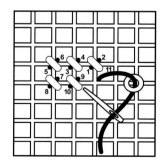

CASHMERE STITCH

This rectangular stitch is formed by working four diagonal stitches as shown in **Fig. 14**.

Fig. 14

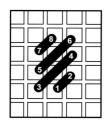

CHECKERED SCOTCH STITCH

This stitch is a combination of Scotch Stitches and Tent Stitches that form a checkerboard pattern **(Fig. 15)**.

Fig. 15

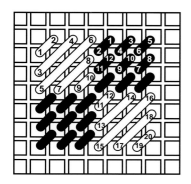

COUCHING

This stitch is composed of one long stitch held in place by vertical tie-down stitches **(Fig. 16)**.

Fig. 16

CROSS STITCH

This stitch is composed of two stitches **(Fig. 17)**. The top stitch of each cross must always be made in the same direction. The number of intersections may vary according to the chart.

Fig. 17

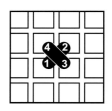

DOUBLE CROSS STITCH VARIATION

This stitch is composed of four stitches **(Fig. 18)**. The top stitch of each cross must always be made in the same direction.

Fig. 18

DOUBLE LEVIATHAN STITCH

This stitch is worked over four threads and is composed of eight stitches, all crossing at the center **(Fig. 19)**.

Fig. 19

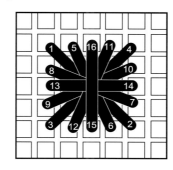

FRENCH KNOT

Bring needle up through hole. Wrap yarn once around needle and insert needle in same hole or adjacent hole, holding end of yarn with non-stitching fingers **(Fig. 20)**. Tighten knot; then pull needle through canvas, holding yarn until it must be released.

Fig. 20

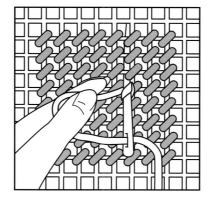

FRINGE

Fold a 12" length of yarn in half. Thread needle with loose ends of yarn. Take needle down at 1, leaving a 1" loop on top of the canvas. Come up at 2, bring needle through loop, and pull tightly **(Fig. 21)**.

Fig. 21

GOBELIN STITCH

This basic straight stitch is worked over two or more threads or intersections. The number of threads or intersections may vary according to the chart **(Fig. 22)**.

Fig. 22

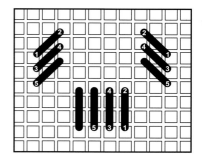

MOSAIC STITCH

This three-stitch pattern forms small squares **(Fig. 23)**.

Fig. 23

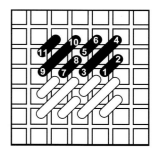

OVERCAST STITCH

This stitch covers the edge of the canvas and joins pieces of canvas **(Fig. 24)**. It may be necessary to go through the same hole more than once to get an even coverage on the edge, especially at the corners.

Fig. 24

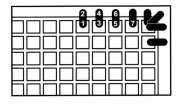

SCOTCH STITCH

This stitch forms a square. It may be worked over three or more horizontal threads by three or more vertical threads. **Fig. 25** shows it worked over three threads.

Fig. 25

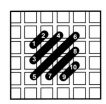

SMYRNA CROSS STITCH

This stitch is worked over two threads as a decorative stitch. Each stitch is worked completely before going on to the next **(Fig. 26)**.

Fig. 26

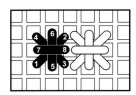

TENT STITCH

This stitch is worked in vertical or horizontal rows over one intersection as shown in **Fig. 27**. Follow **Fig. 28** to work the **Reversed Tent Stitch**. Sometimes when you are working Tent Stitches, the last stitch on the row will look "pulled" on the front of your piece when you are changing directions. To avoid this problem, leave a loop of yarn on the wrong side of the stitched piece after making the last stitch in the row. When making the first stitch in the next row, run your needle through the loop **(Fig. 29)**. Gently pull yarn until all stitches are even.

Fig. 27

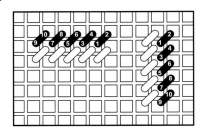

Fig. 28

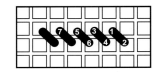

Fig. 29

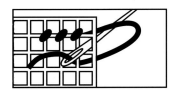

TURKEY LOOP STITCH

This stitch is composed of locked loops. Bring needle up through hole and back down through same hole, forming a loop on top of the canvas. A locking stitch is then made across the thread directly below or to either side of loop as shown in **Fig. 30**.

Fig. 30

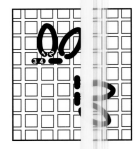

UPRIGHT CROSS STITCH

This stitch is worked over two threads as shown in **Fig. 31**. The top stitch of each cross must always be made in the same direction.

Fig. 31

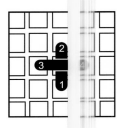

Instructions tested and photography items made by Janet Akins, Kathleen Boyd, Virginia Cates, Sharl Dunigan, JoAnn Forrest, Christel Shelton and Janie Wright.

INDEX

INDEX (Continued)

 O

 P–R

 S

 T–W